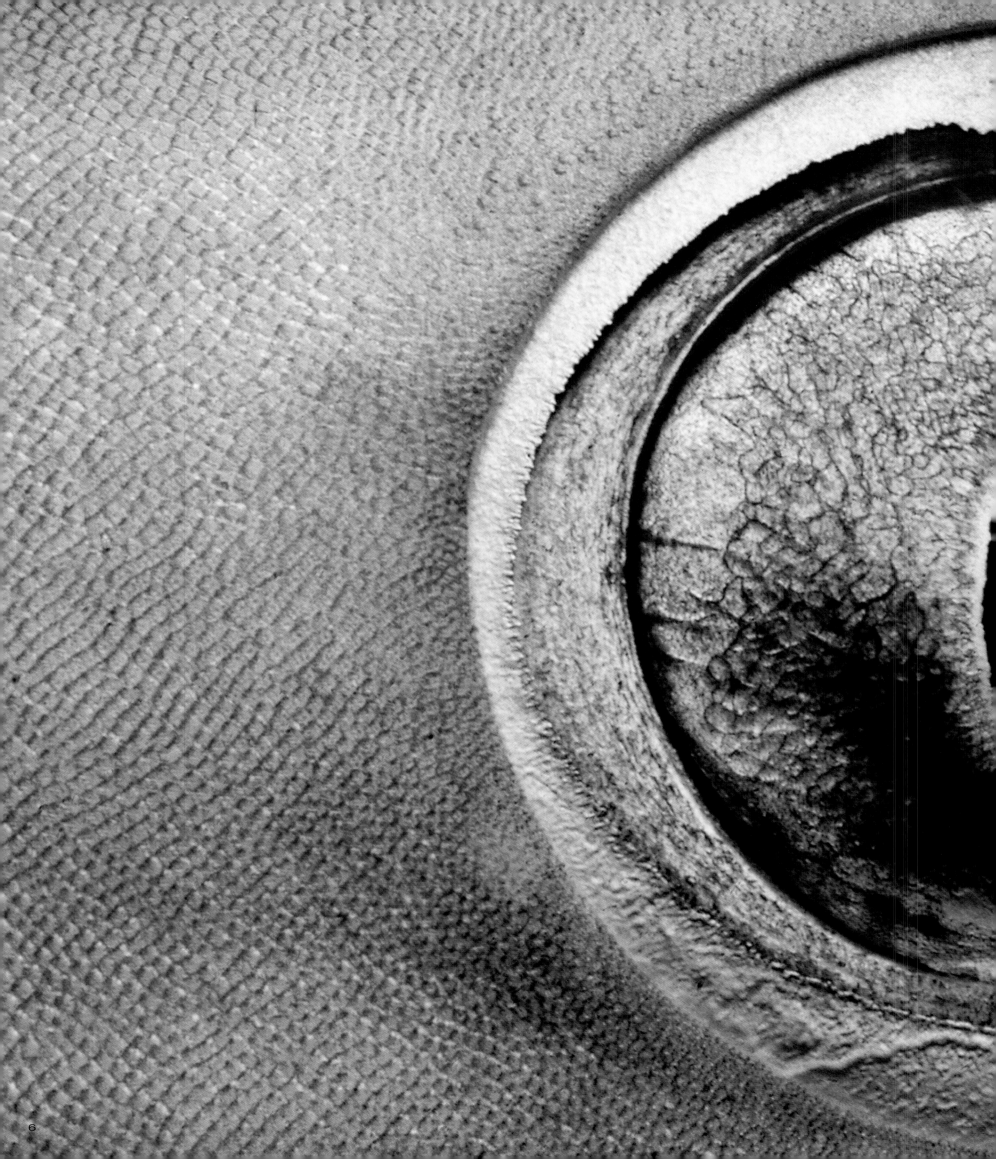

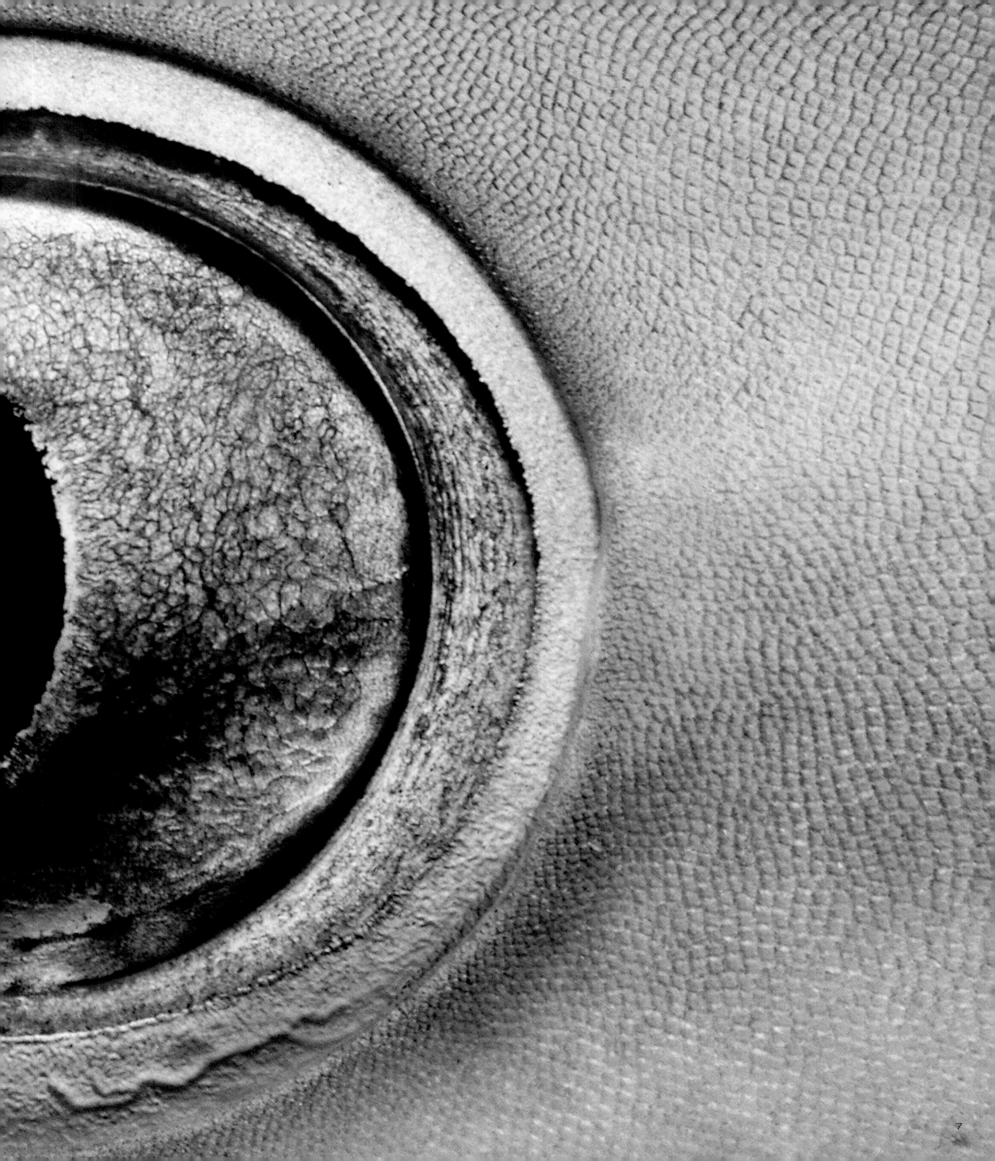

SHARK!

Jeffrey L. Rotman

ipso facto
PUBLISHERS • NYC

Photographing Sharks

When people find out that I am a professional underwater photographer, they inevitably ask, How do you avoid sharks? My answer: Jump in the water with a camera! Sharks are among the most elusive, frustrating subjects to photograph. Far from stalking human prey, the strange sight of a wetsuited diver trailing a stream of bubbles causes most to turn tail and run. Consequently, patience and luck are major factors in locating sharks in the sea. These photographs are gleaned from thousands of hours underwater over 25 years of diving.

Although countless hours spent in the sharks environment will eventually yield some chance encounters, experience has taught me that I need to target a certain species in order to capture it on film. To guarantee a meeting I need to take into

account the particular sharks seasonal migration, its preferred prey, and the depth it frequents.

Food is often an enticement to get sharks to approach and overcome their fears of my presence. At times, it works all too well. Once while chumming for Caribbean reef sharks in the Bahamas we attracted in the neighborhood of 30 sharks. As they swarmed around my lens, I felt like a fashion photographer, shooting provocative poses as fast as I could focus my camera. Then without warning the sharks fled as one. I turned around to confront the largest hammerhead I had ever seen. Foolishly, I was in the open ocean without a safety diver. No dive buddy, no coral reef to back into, no antishark device to defend myself. The beast made one pass, probably decided

In the sixties, the shark cage was developed to allow photographers to work safely around great white sharks. The shark cage is very effective as long as you stay inside the cage. An incidental benefit turned out to be that the metal bars seem to excite the magnetic perception of sharks and draw them to the cages. In the 1980s the chainmail shark suit was developed so that divers could leave the safety of the cage and get inside a pack of feeding sharks to take dramatic close-ups. It fits over your wet suit and prevents the shark's teeth from penetrating your skin. It allows you to swim freely among sharks and still concentrate on your photography, provided the sharks aren't too large. A big shark can easily crush an arm or leg in its maw, or, once it grabs hold of an arm pull it right out of its socket.

One of the most important criteria in photographing sharks is your ability as a diver. If something does go wrong in the middle of a tense shooting situation your instinctive reactions can and do make the difference. The golden rule is never underestimate the shark and overestimate your abilities as a diver. It stands to reason that the more you work with sharks the better you become in understanding their unspoken language. And sharks definitely speak. Sometimes they yell! Erratic movements indicate excitement. They are often followed by an attempt to get at the object of that excitement. Some sharks arch their backs and lower their pectoral fins before charging. However, it is worth remembering that each shark, much like humans, is an individual with its own attitude, feelings and personality.

I use a variety of film emulsions with different speeds depending on such variables as light, visibility, depth and subject. Natural light is great when you're close to the surface, but that is not always the case. When I do need artificial light I try to use just one flash. For cameras I rely on Nikonos IIIs and Vs and motorized Nikon F3s with action finders in Aquatica III housings. I use a variety of lenses from 16mm fisheyes to macro to get the desired results.

In addition to mountains of expensive equipment, photographing sharks safely requires engaging an experienced captain, a reliable safety diver, and renting a boat big enough to carry you and your equipment. It can be a very costly obsession. However, the public's seemingly insatiable appetite for good shark photography has allowed me to indulge my passion. I know that if I am able to get fresh and revealing shark images there are editors ready to publish my results. Even the most apathetic editor gets excited when I arrive with a good shark story.

Although photographing sharks has been a lifelong passion, each encounter is a breathtaking moment, as surprising and fulfilling as the first time. Each meeting is an unexpected pleasure, like longtime lovers accidentally meeting on the street. My love affair with sharks is a flame that never flickers, and a lifetime underwater has not dampened it.

Jeff Rotman

that I wasn't worth the bother, and casually cruised on by. I got myself back in the boat FAST.
Your invitation to dine may also bring in some unintended guests. While you might be chumming for reef sharks, the appearance of a few 4-meter tiger sharks can make your pulse race. When excited by food, sharks can move at alarming speeds in unpredictable and erratic ways. You, on the other hand, have a lot of cumbersome dive gear that makes your reactions slow and clumsy. One powerful thrust of the tail can put that shark on top of you before there is time to react. Trying to keep track of the situation with more than one hungry shark can very quickly develop into an emergency.
There have been numerous antishark devices developed throughout the years to deal with over eager sharks. Some even work! Possibly the oldest, and one that is very effective in the right hands, is the shark billy. A shark billy is a sawed off baseball bat with spikes protruding from one end. When applied to the sensitive snout of an aggressive shark, the animal instantly understands and responds to the warning.

One In The Sea

Close-Ups

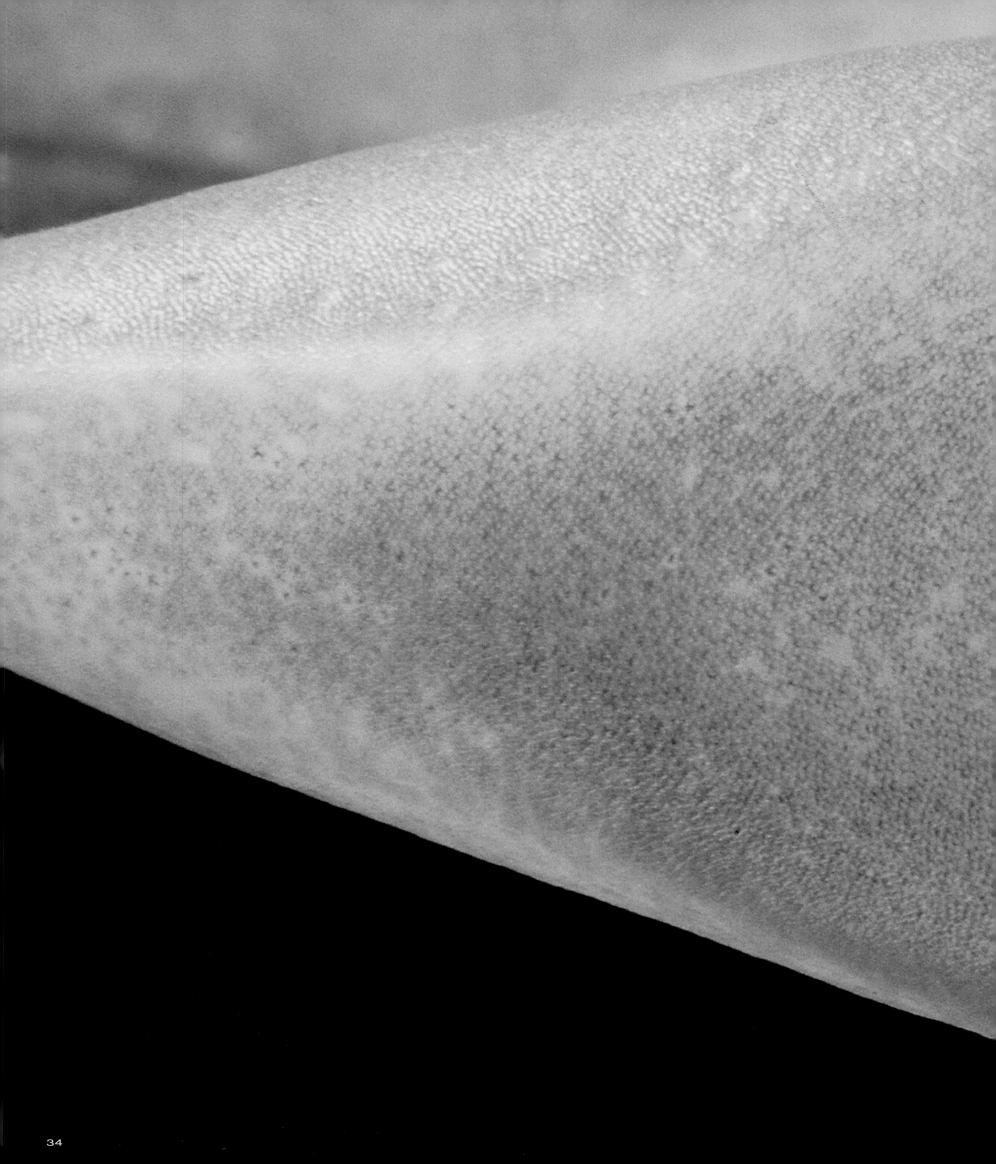

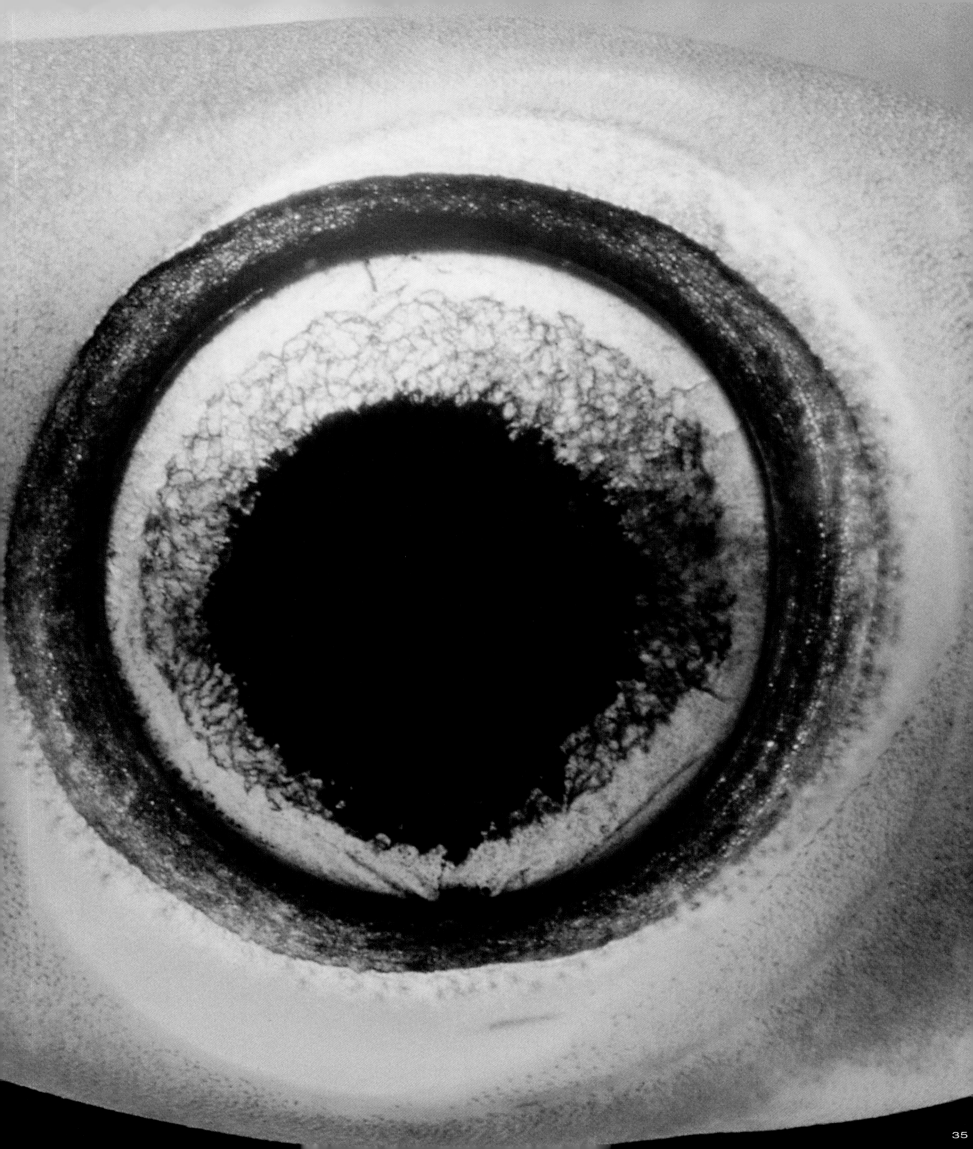

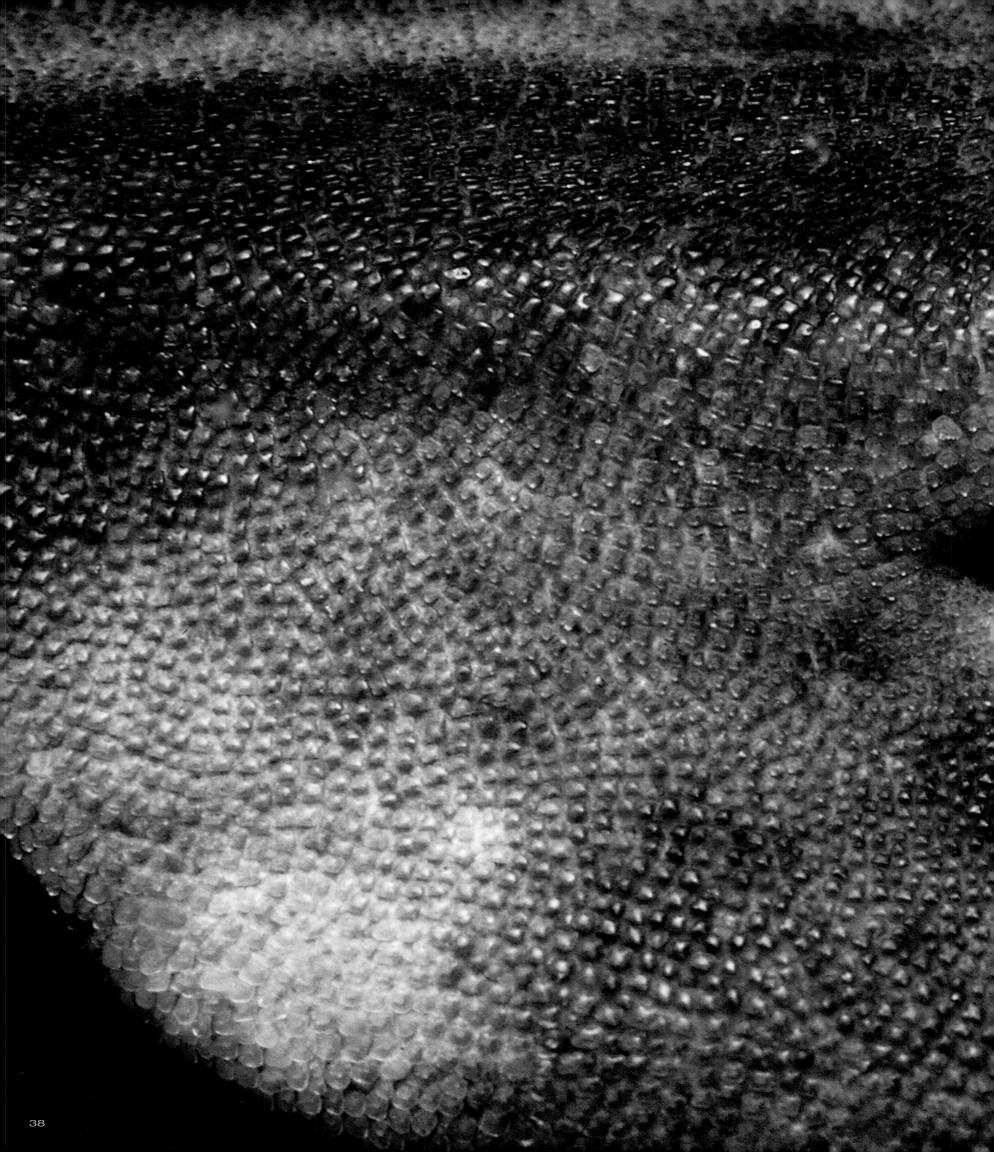

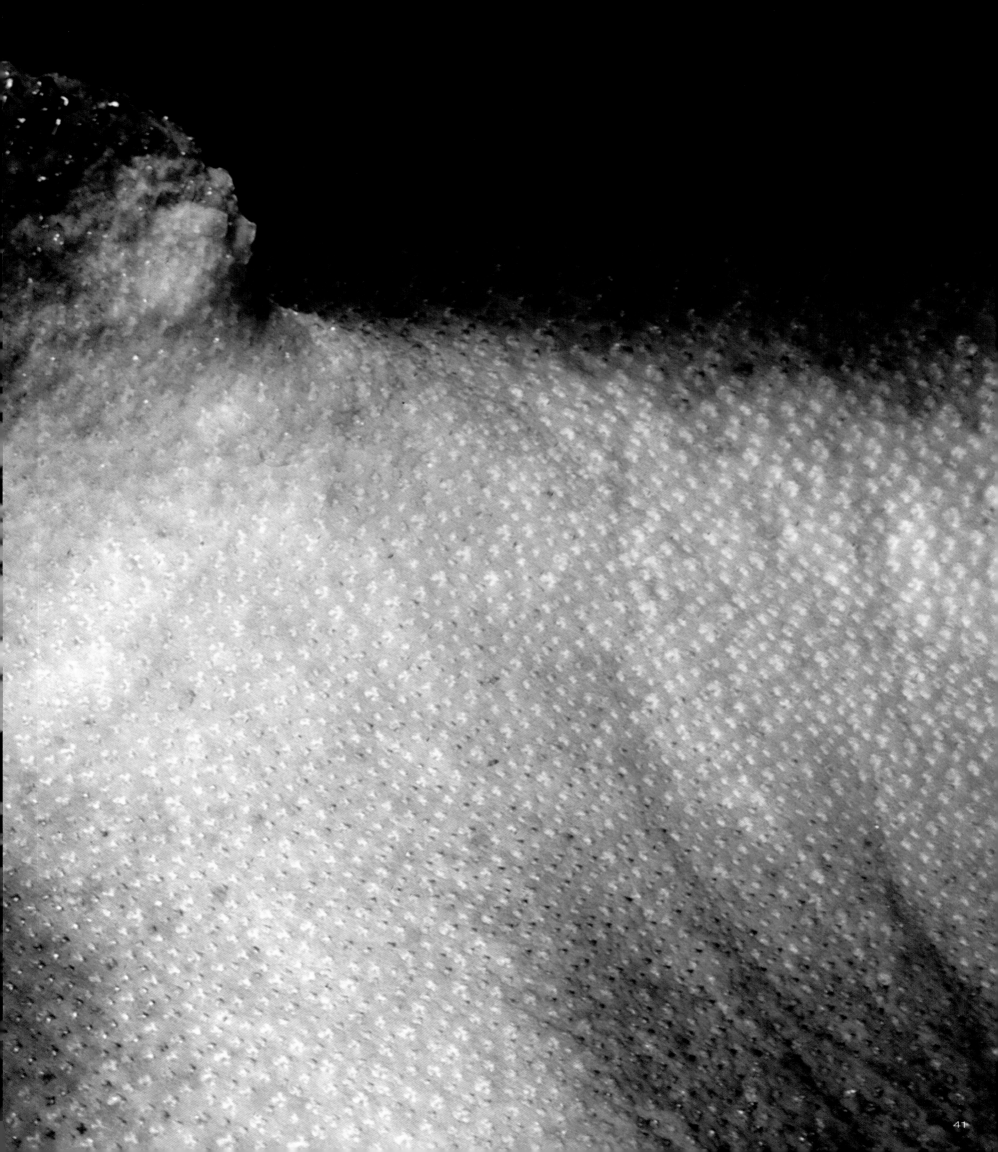

41

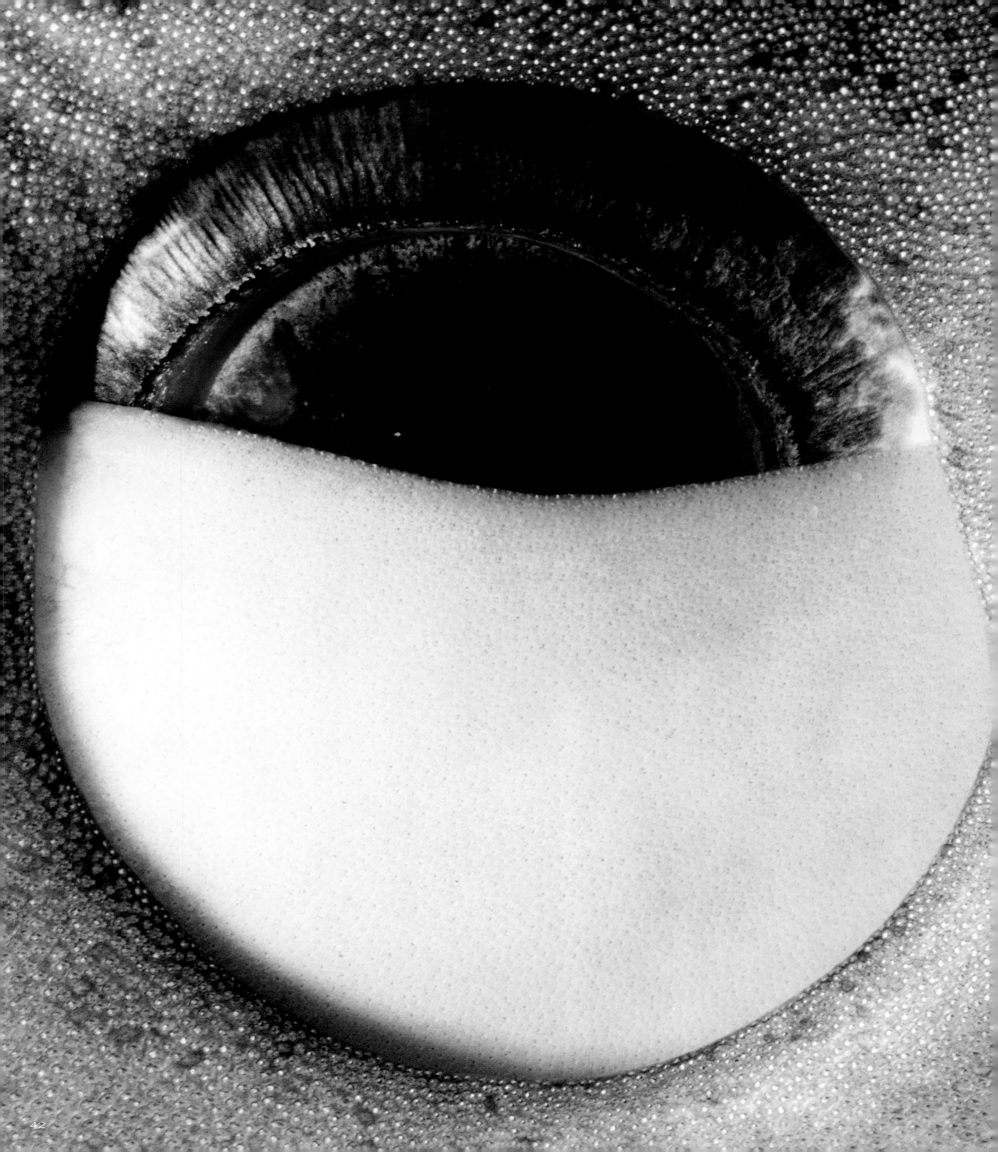

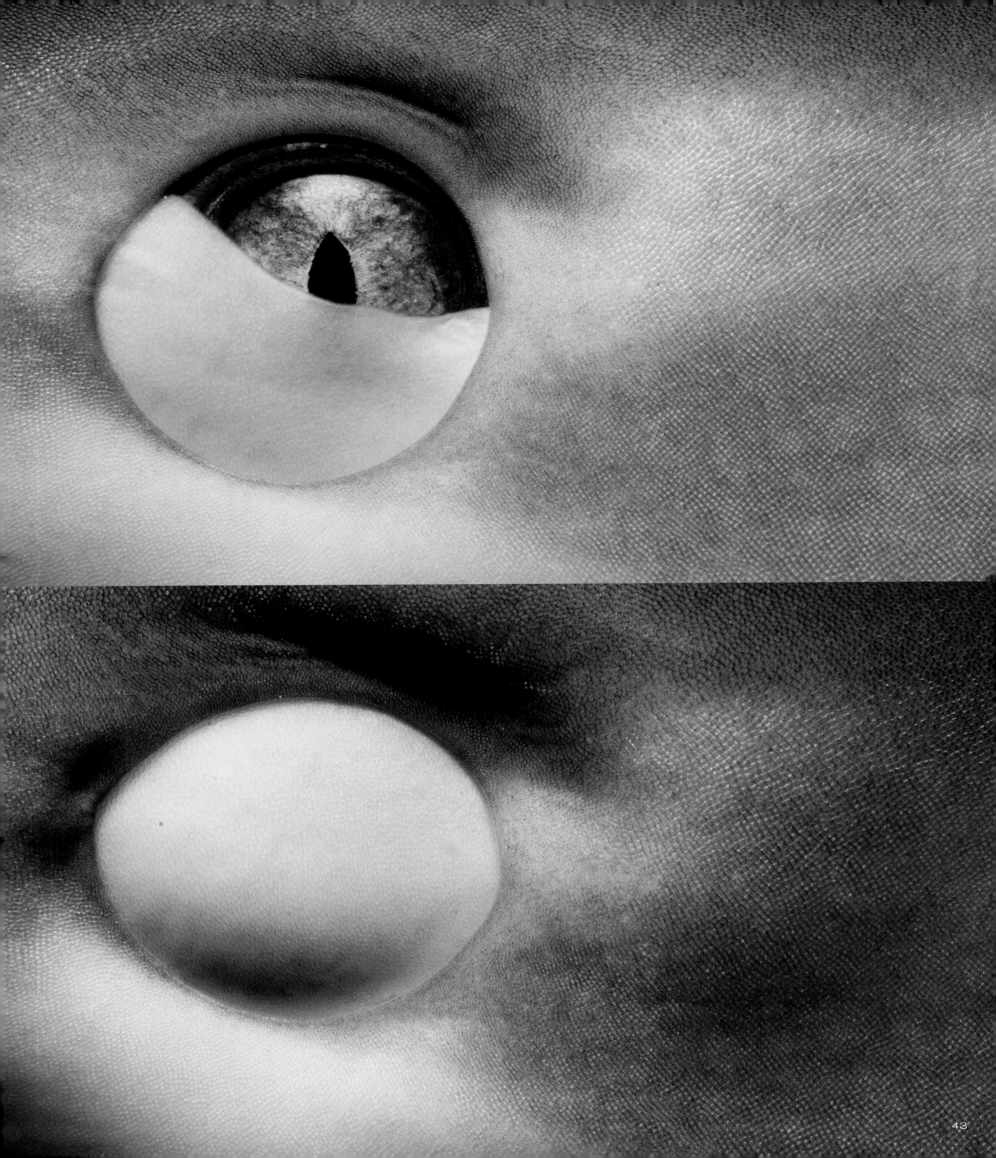

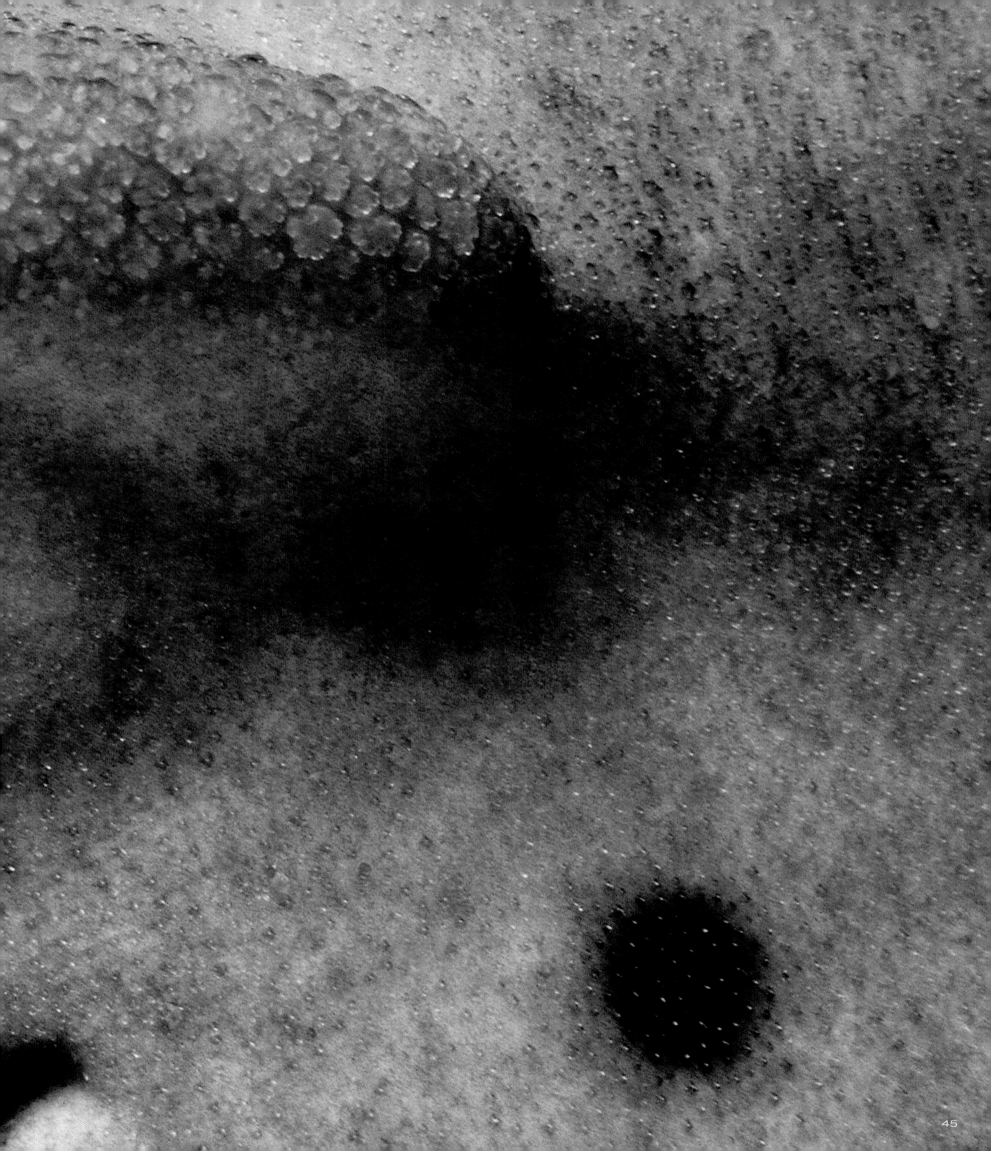

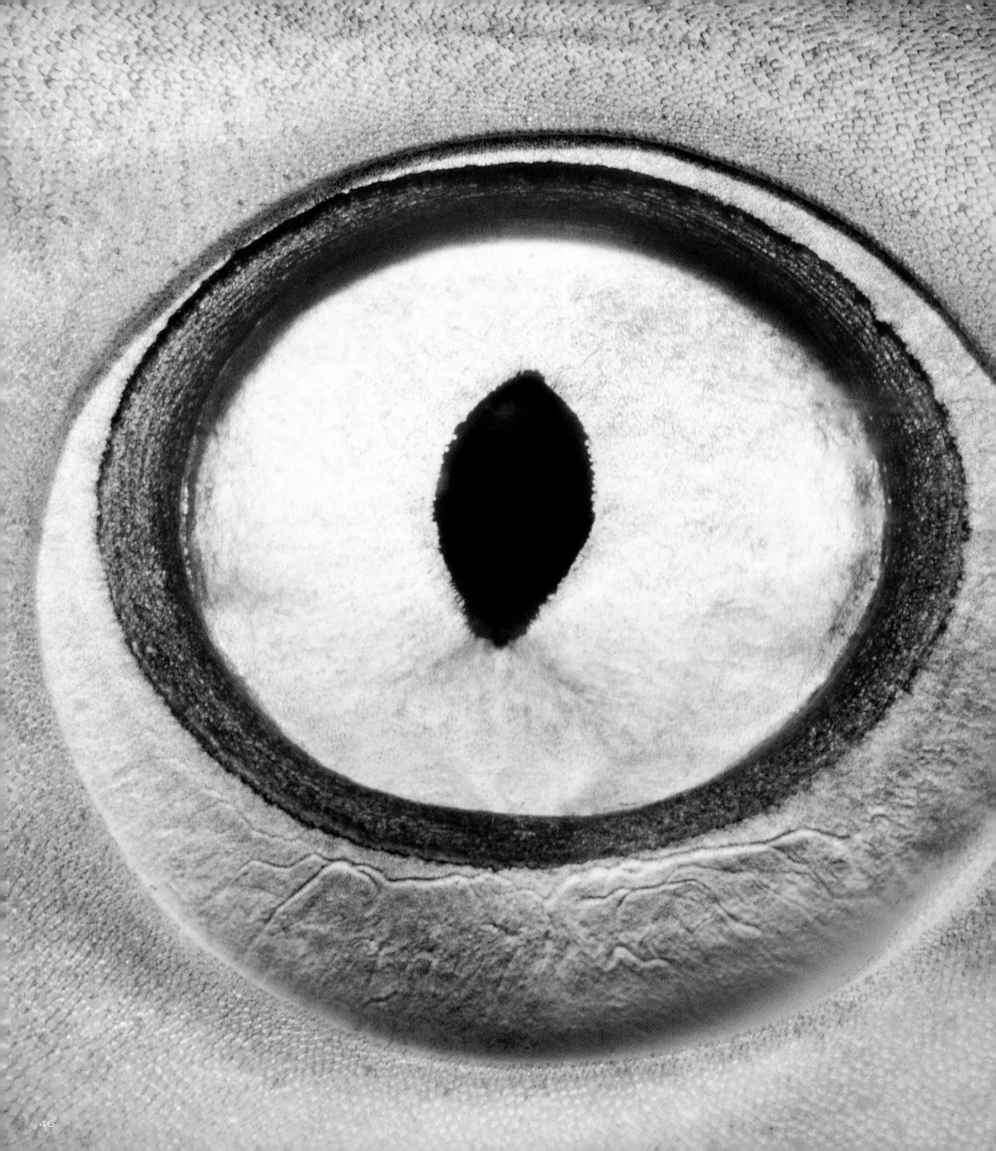

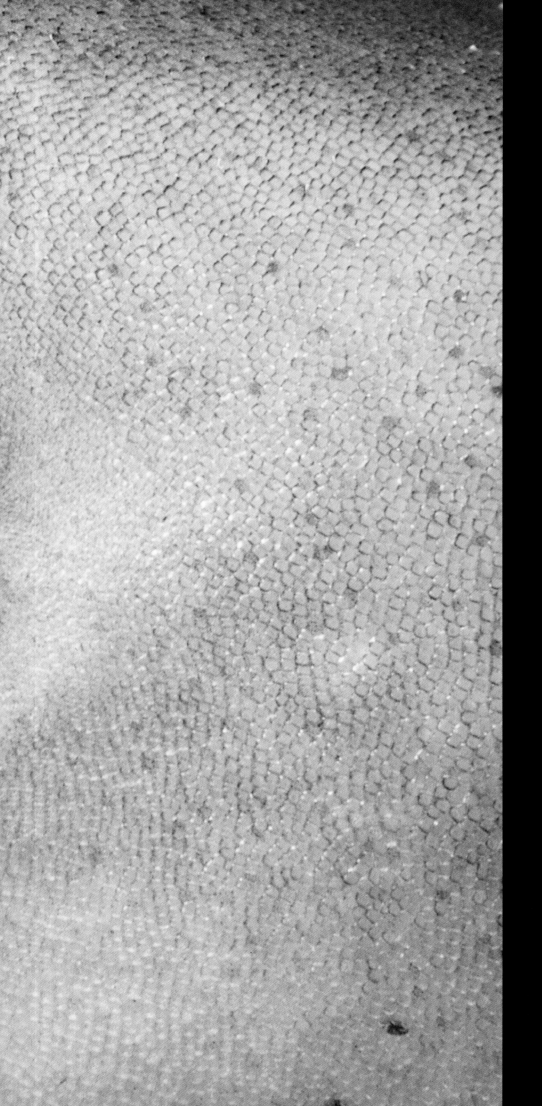

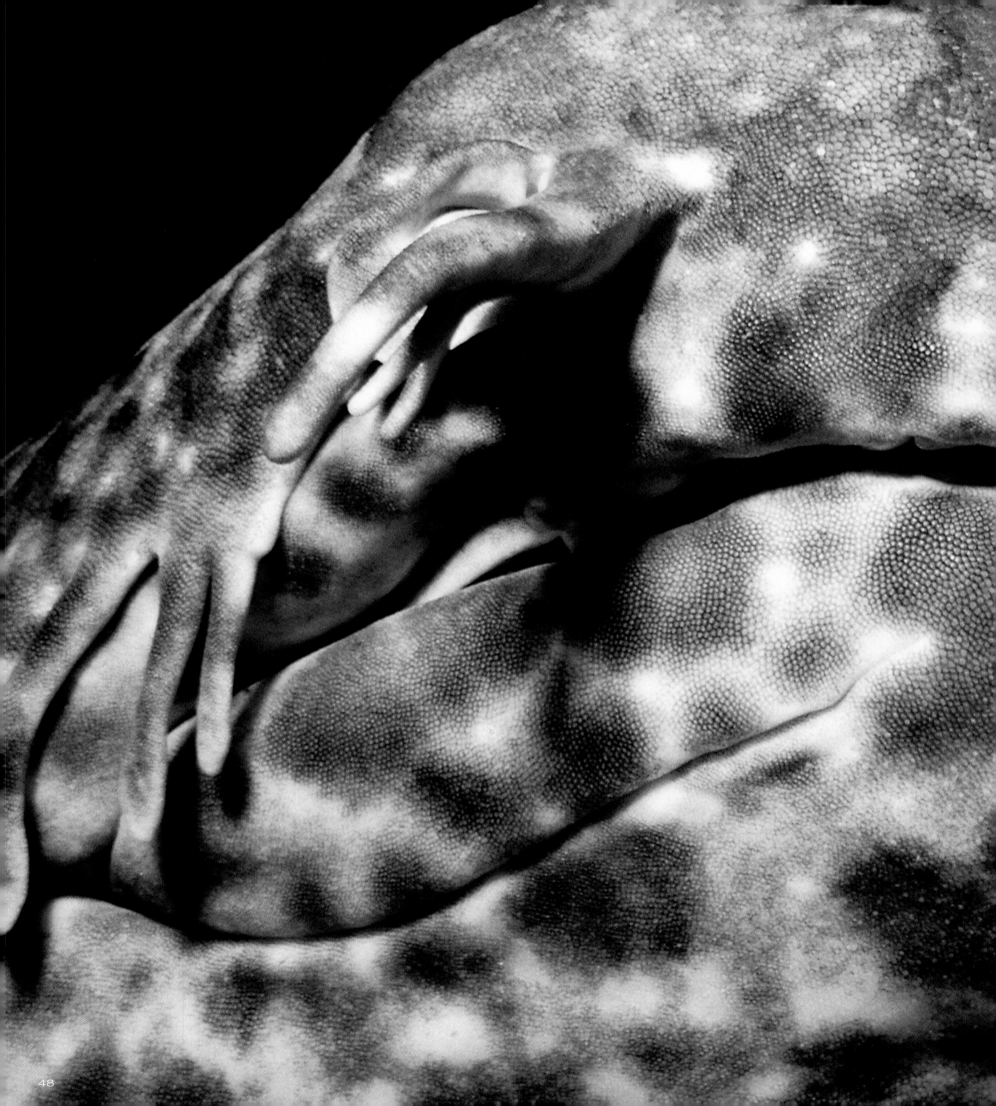

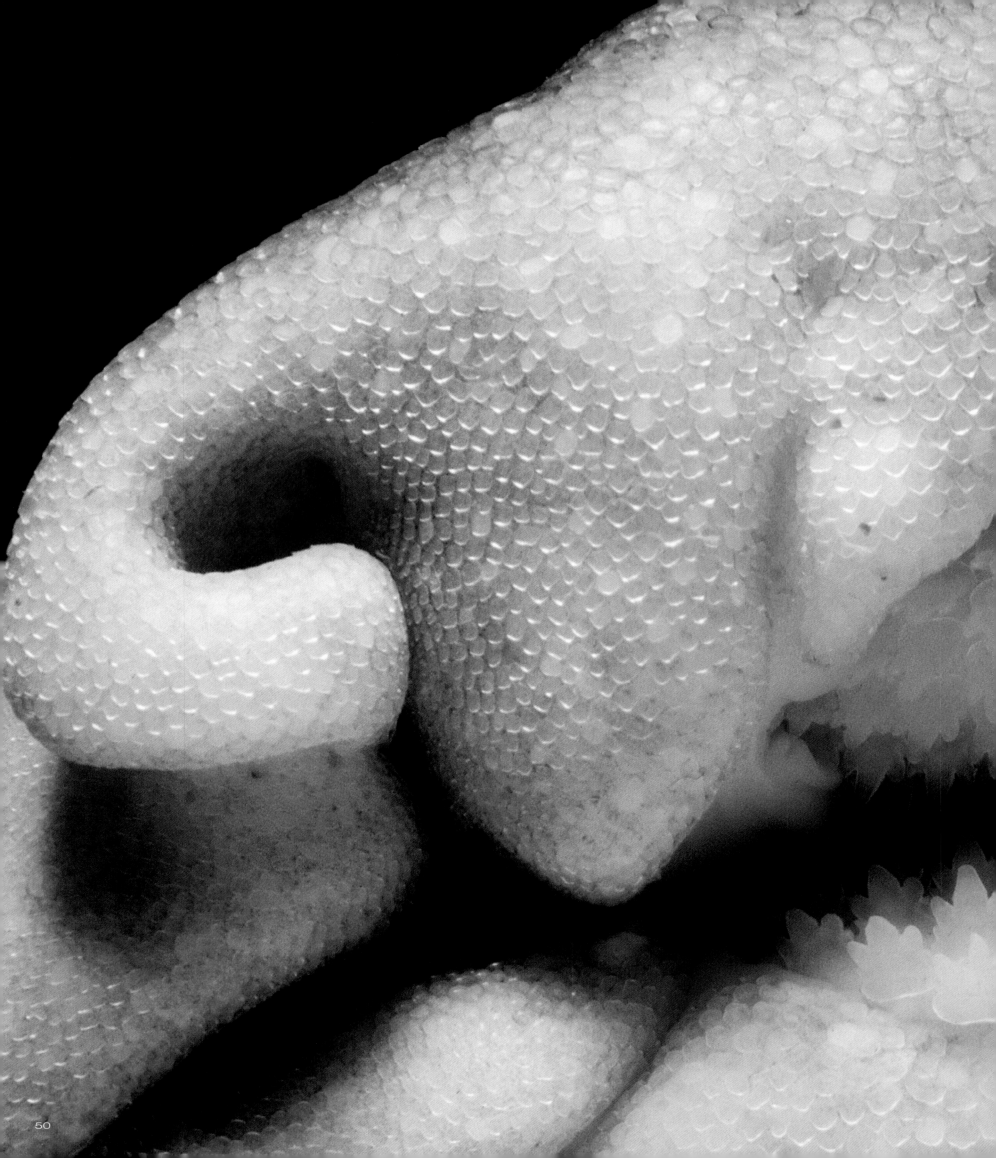

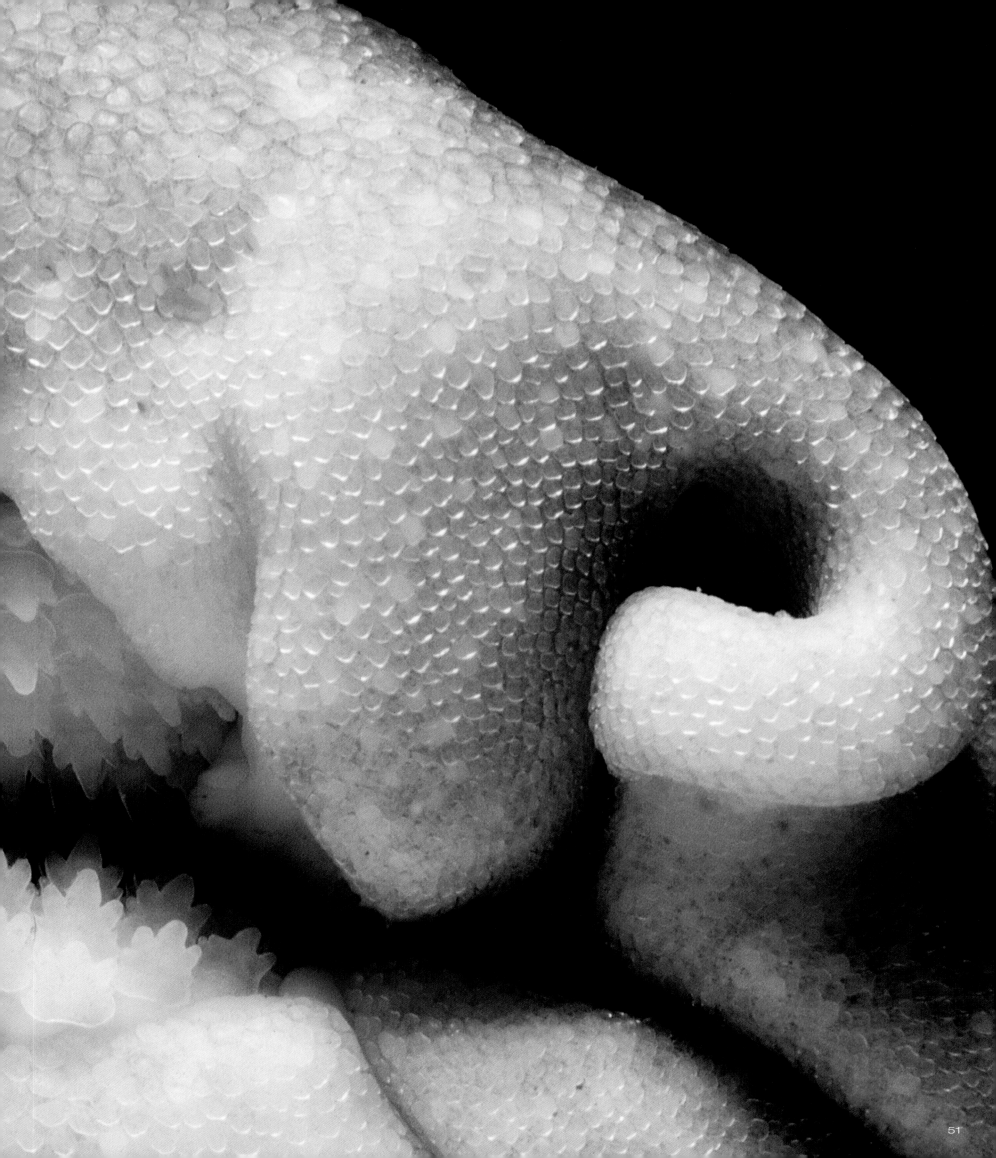

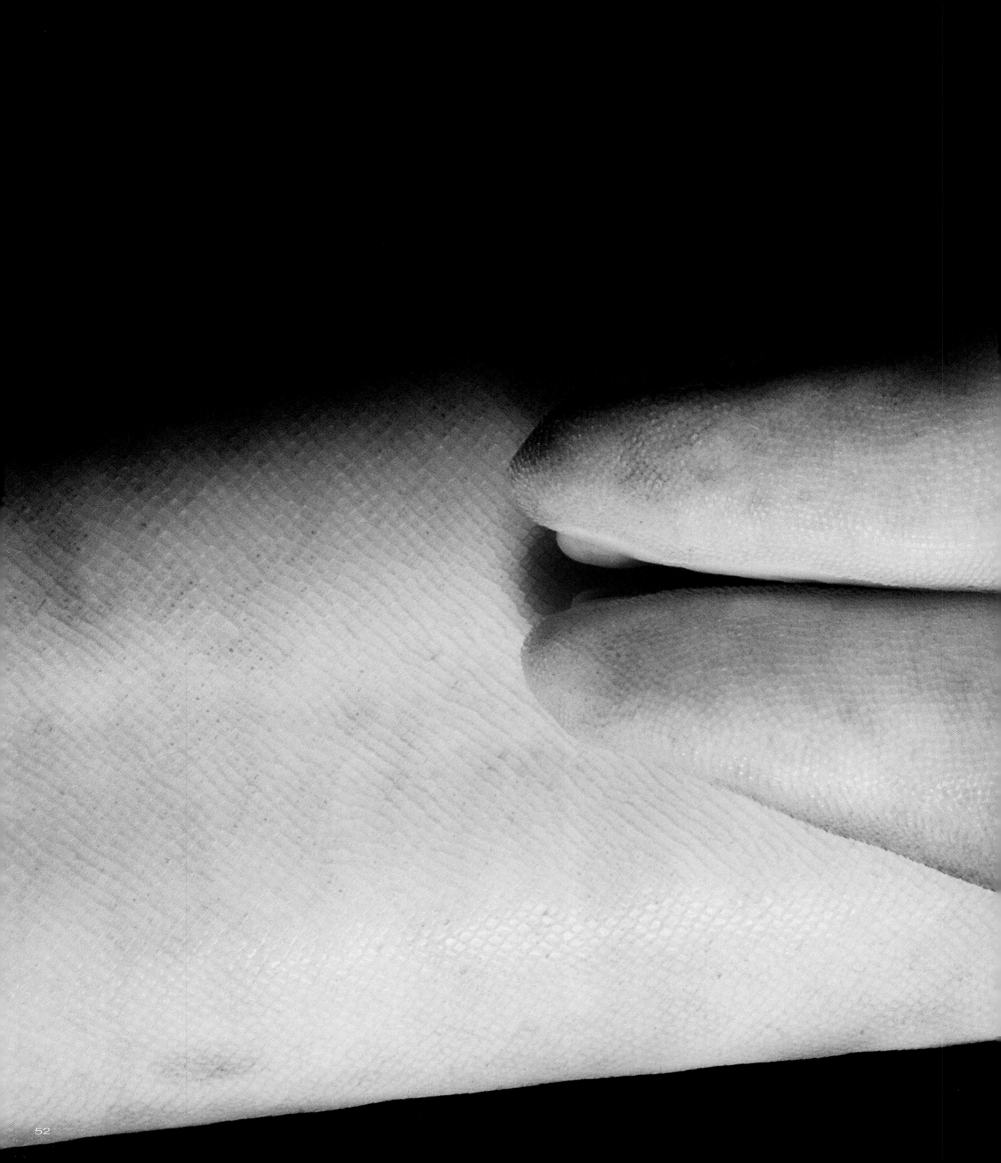

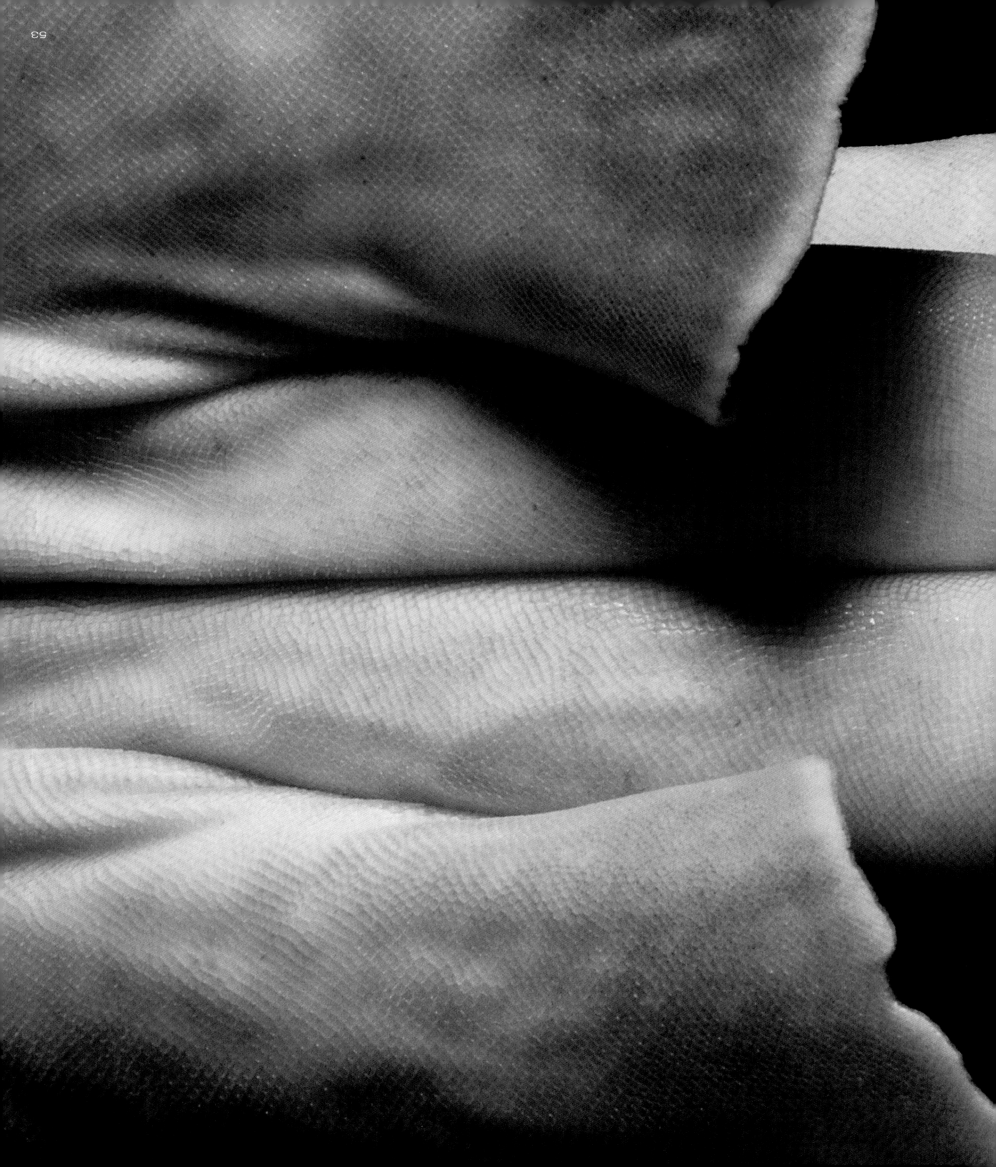

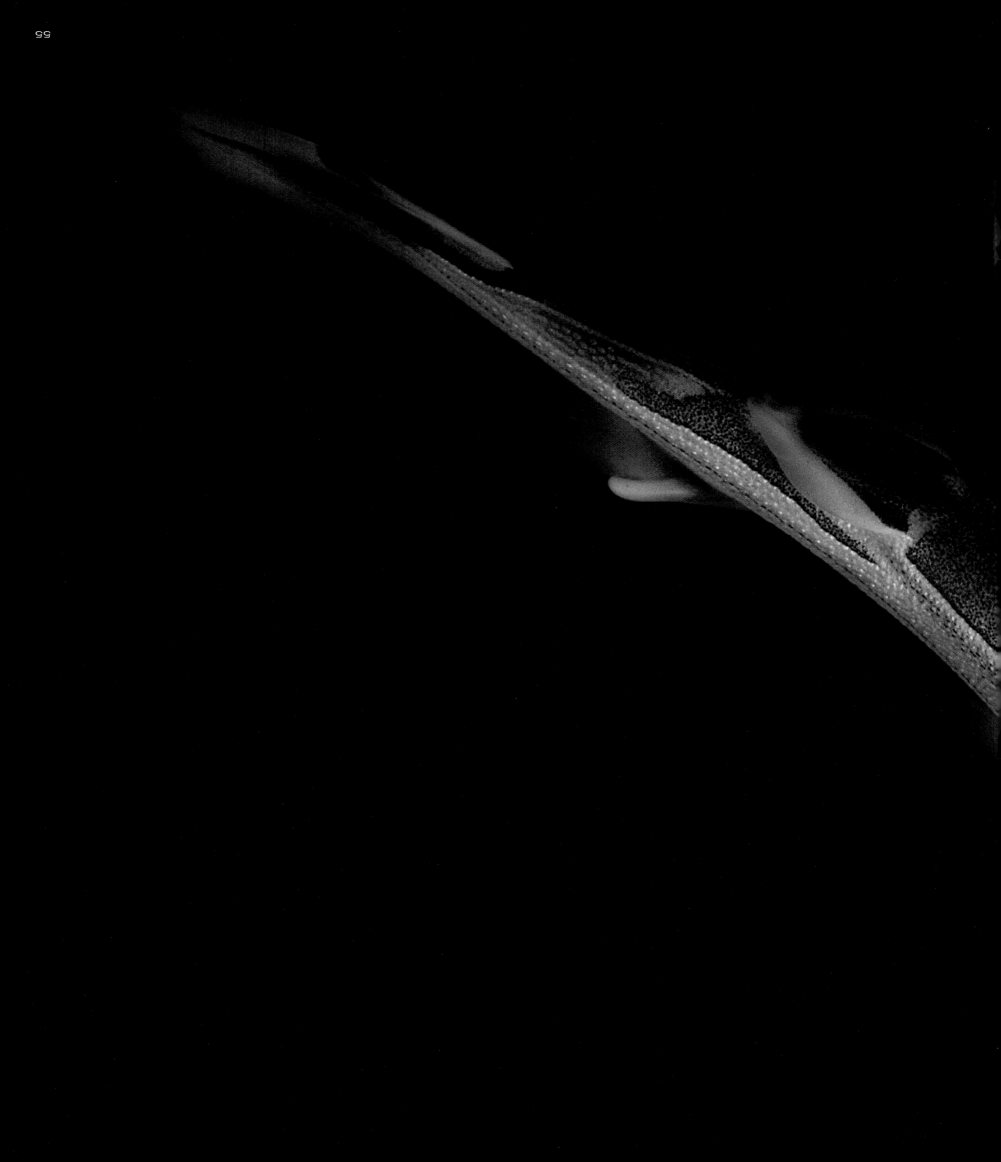

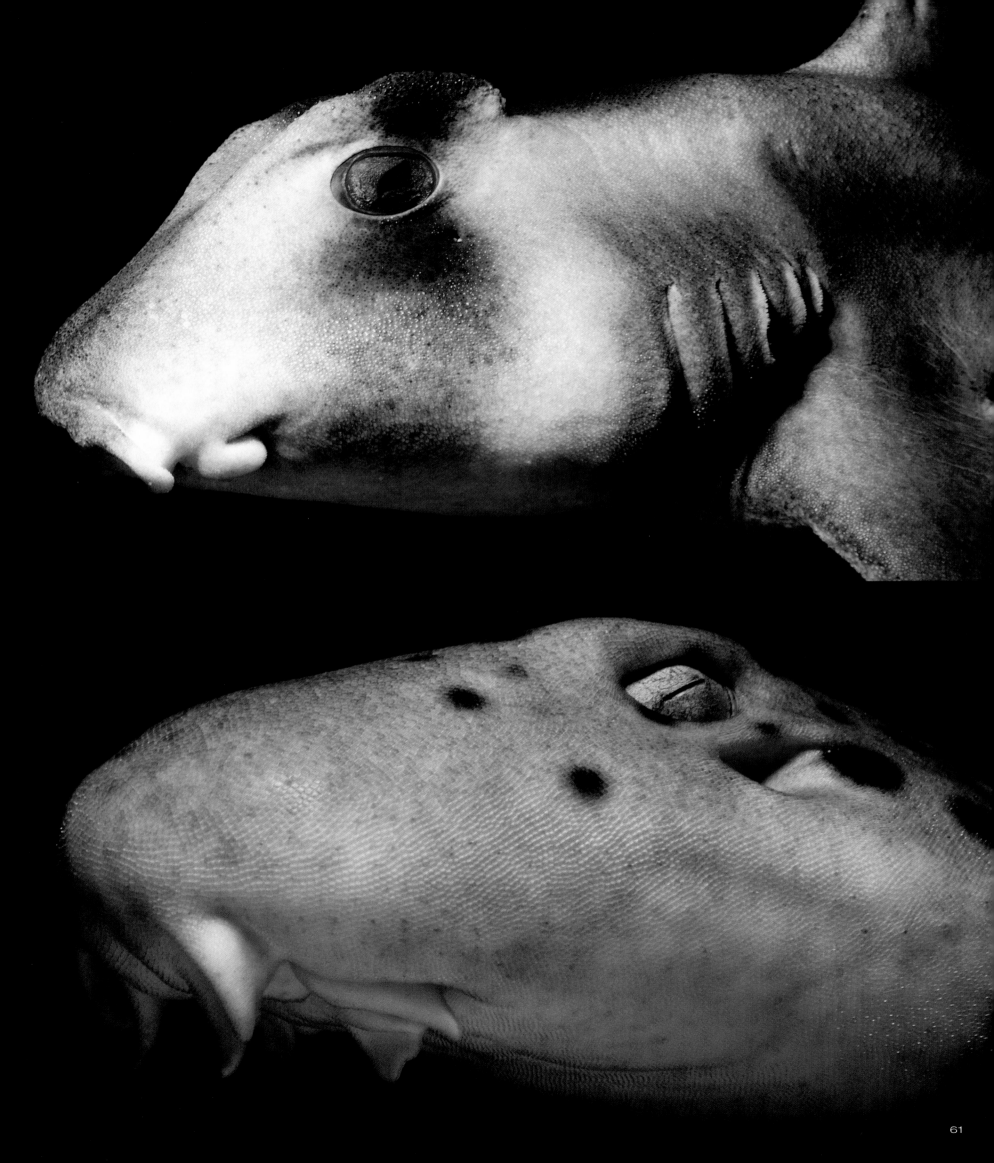

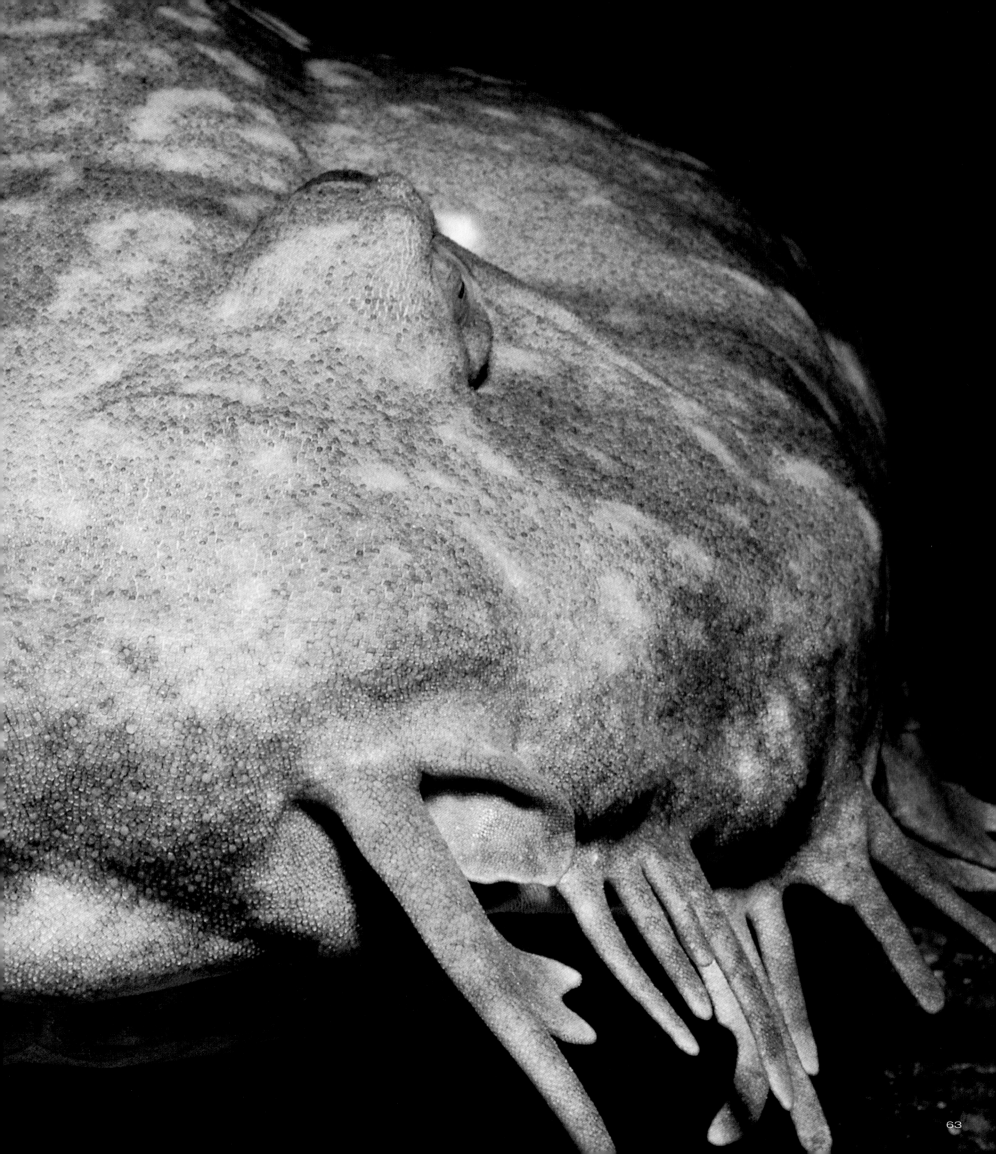

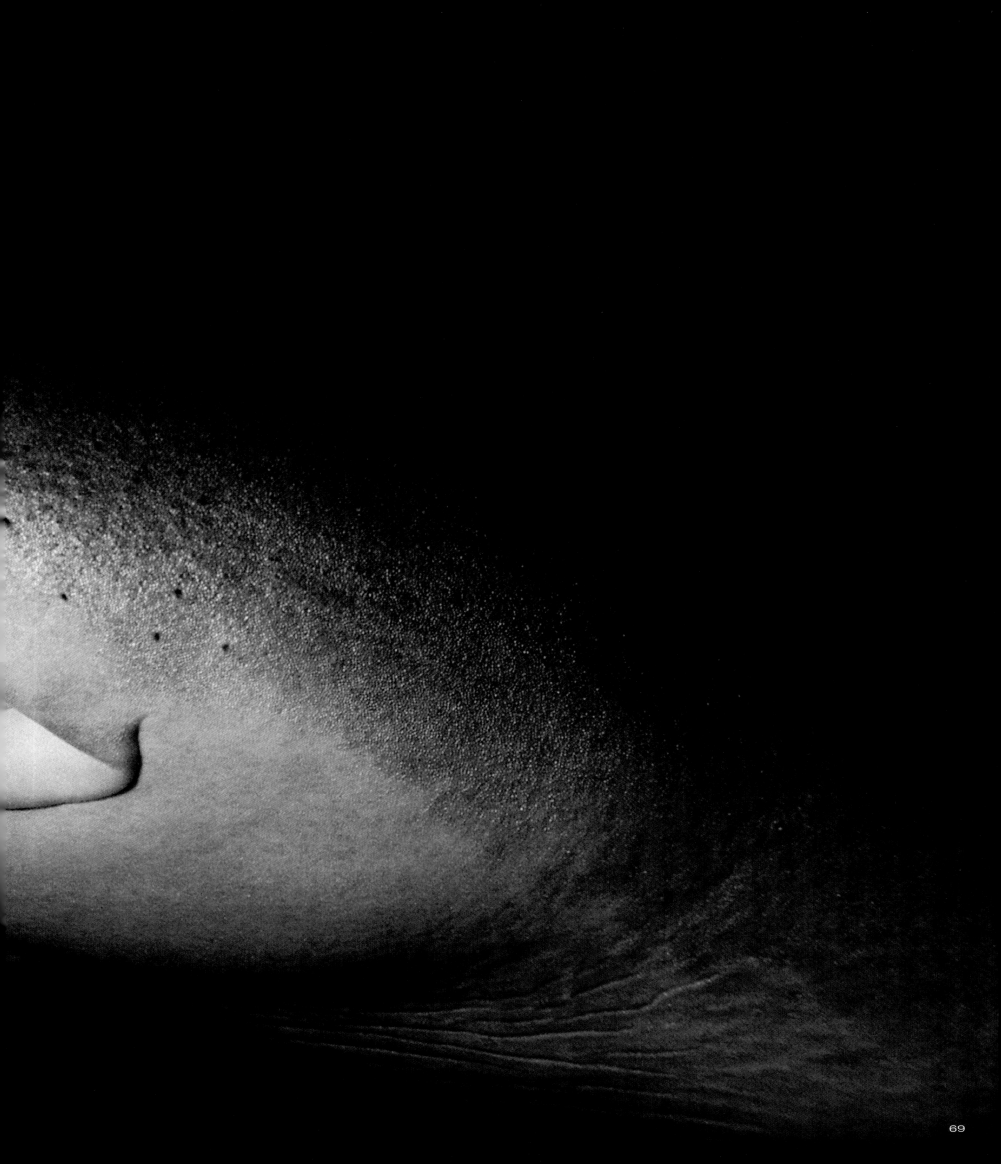

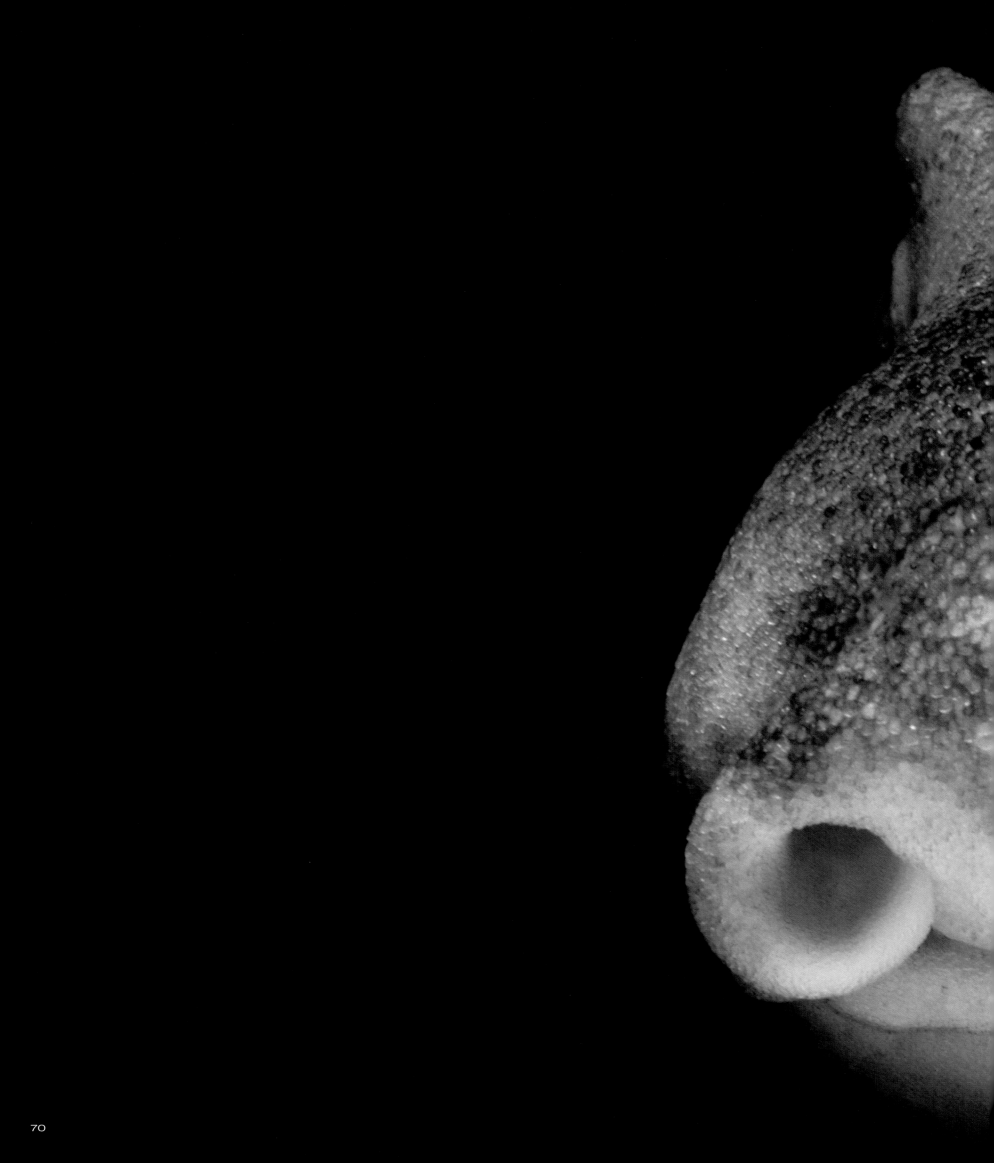

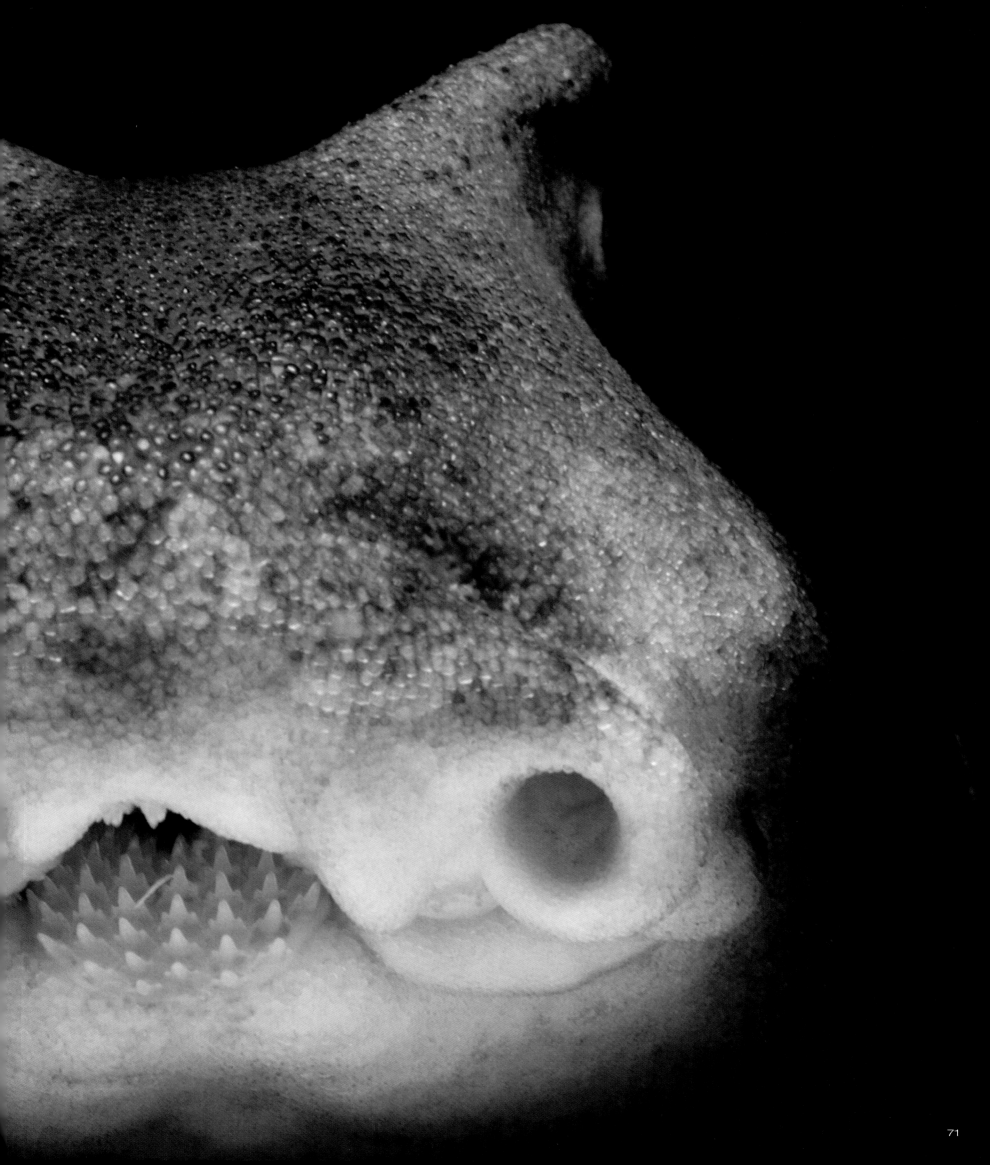

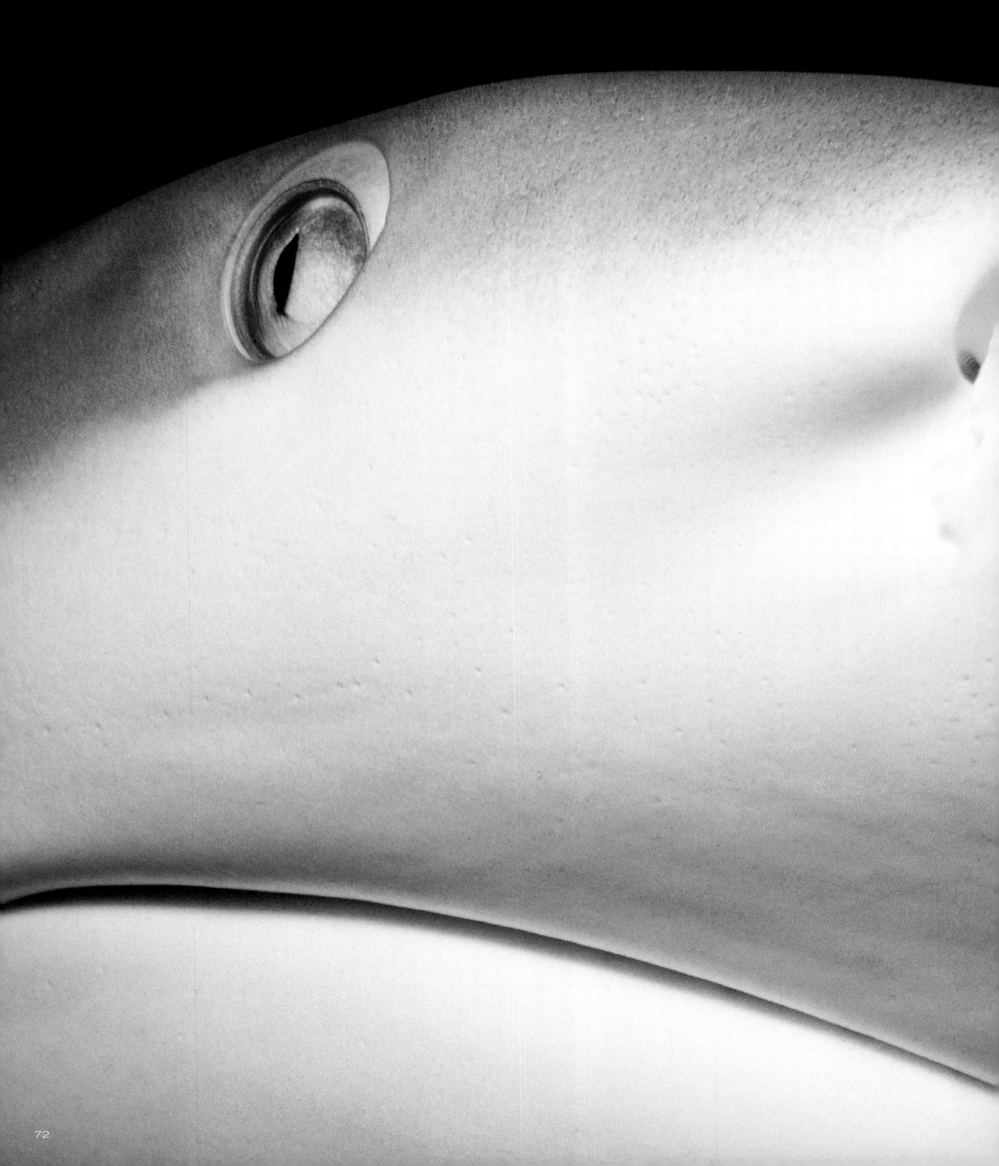

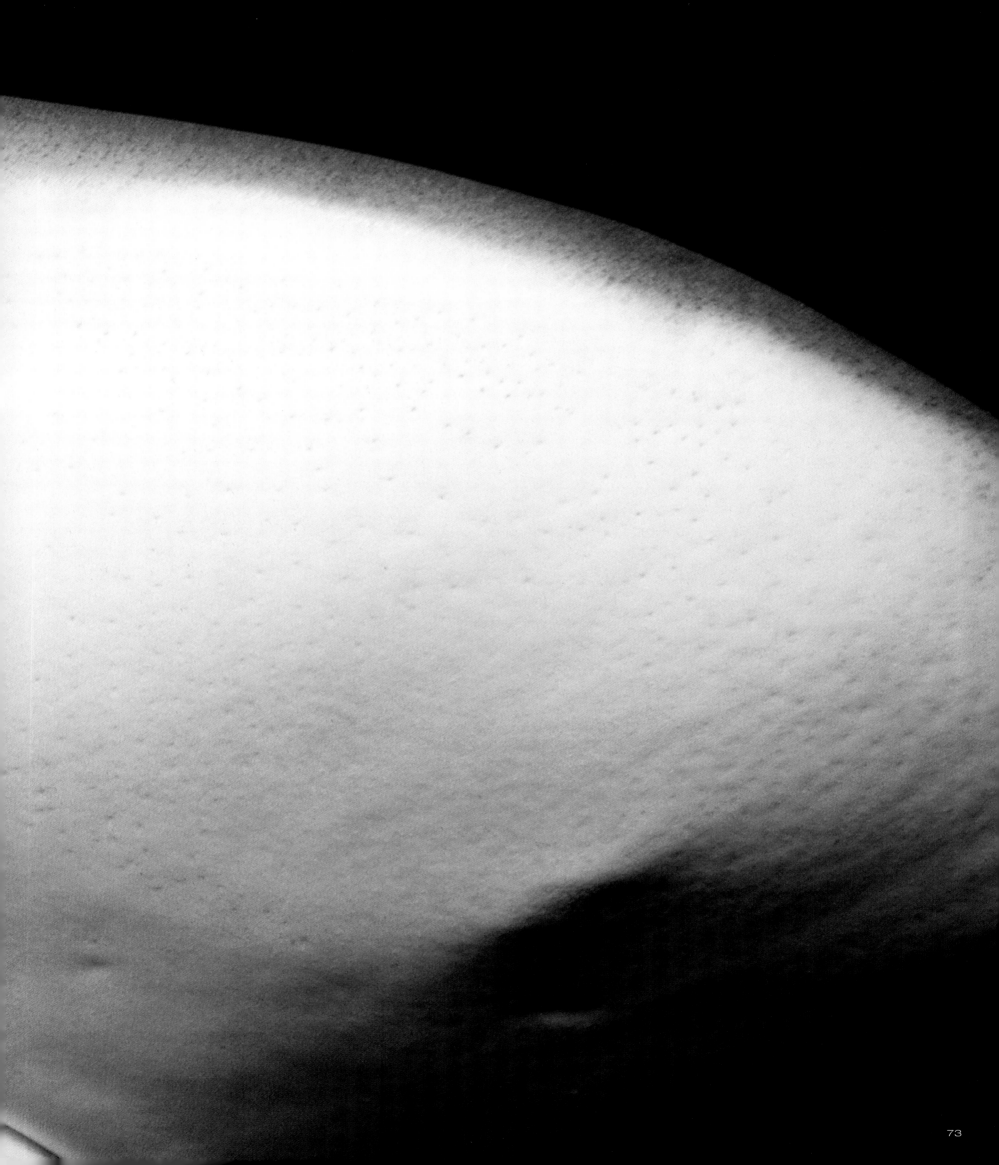

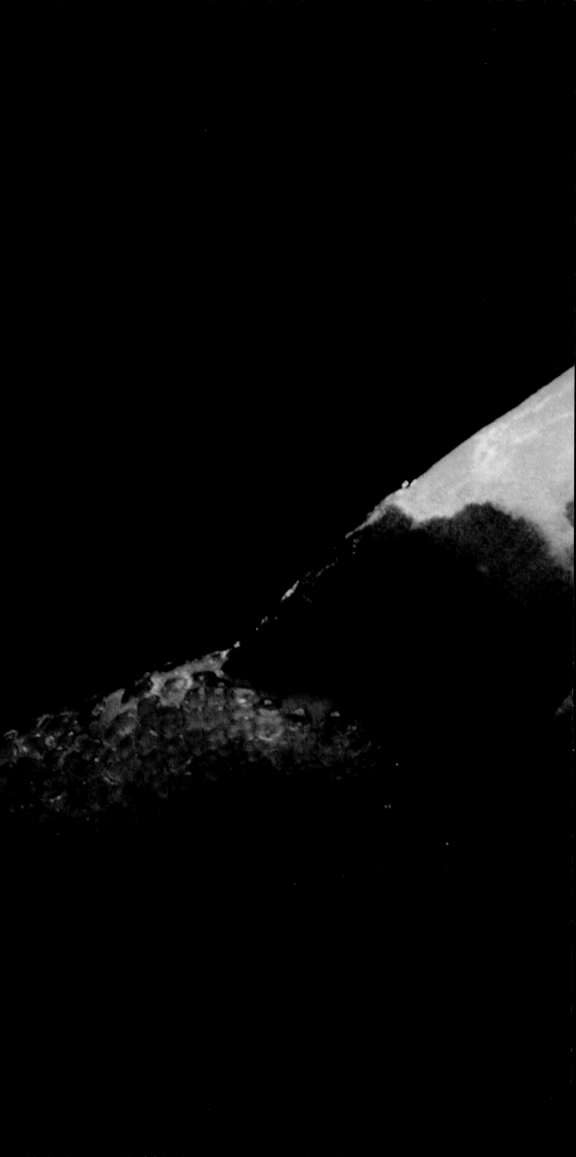

Giants

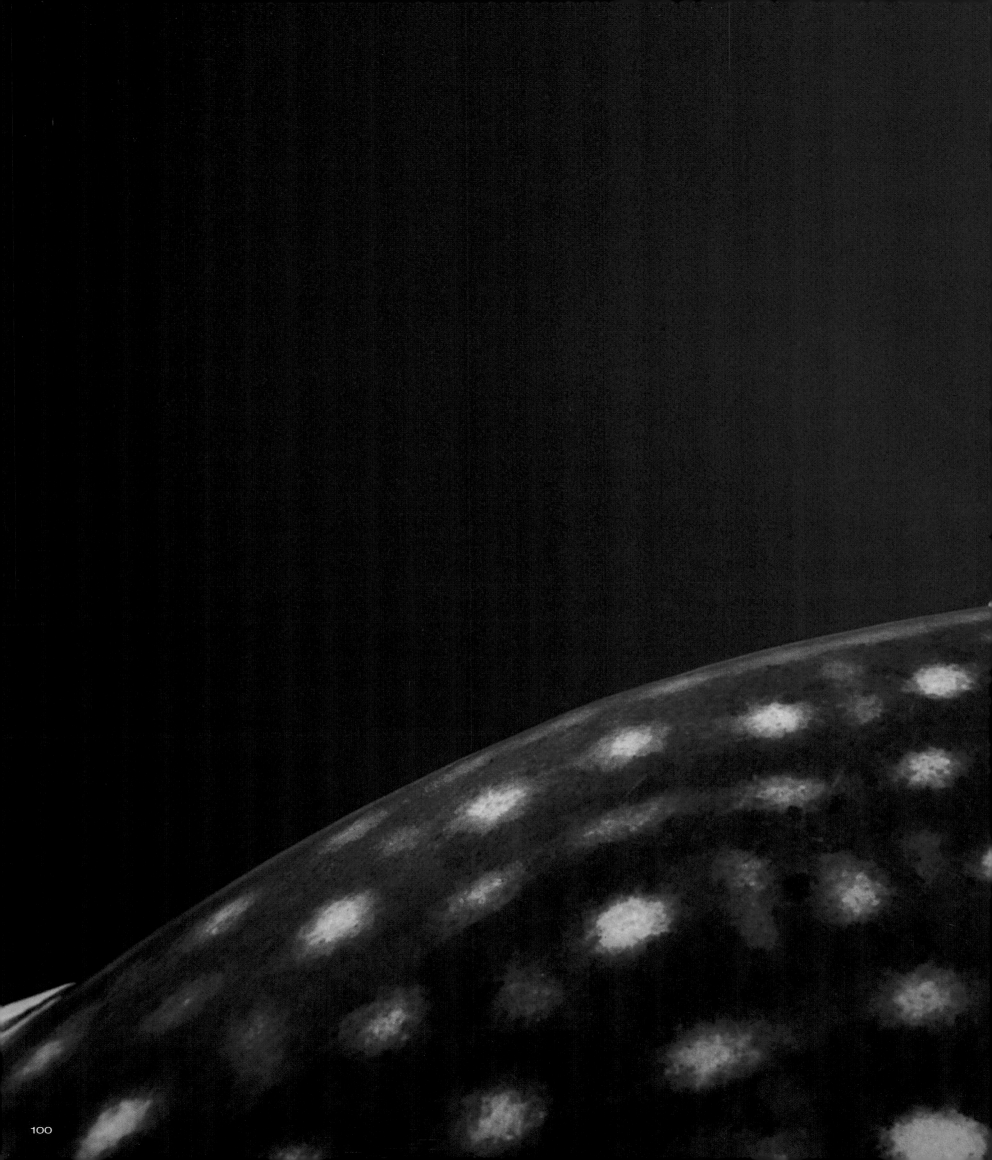

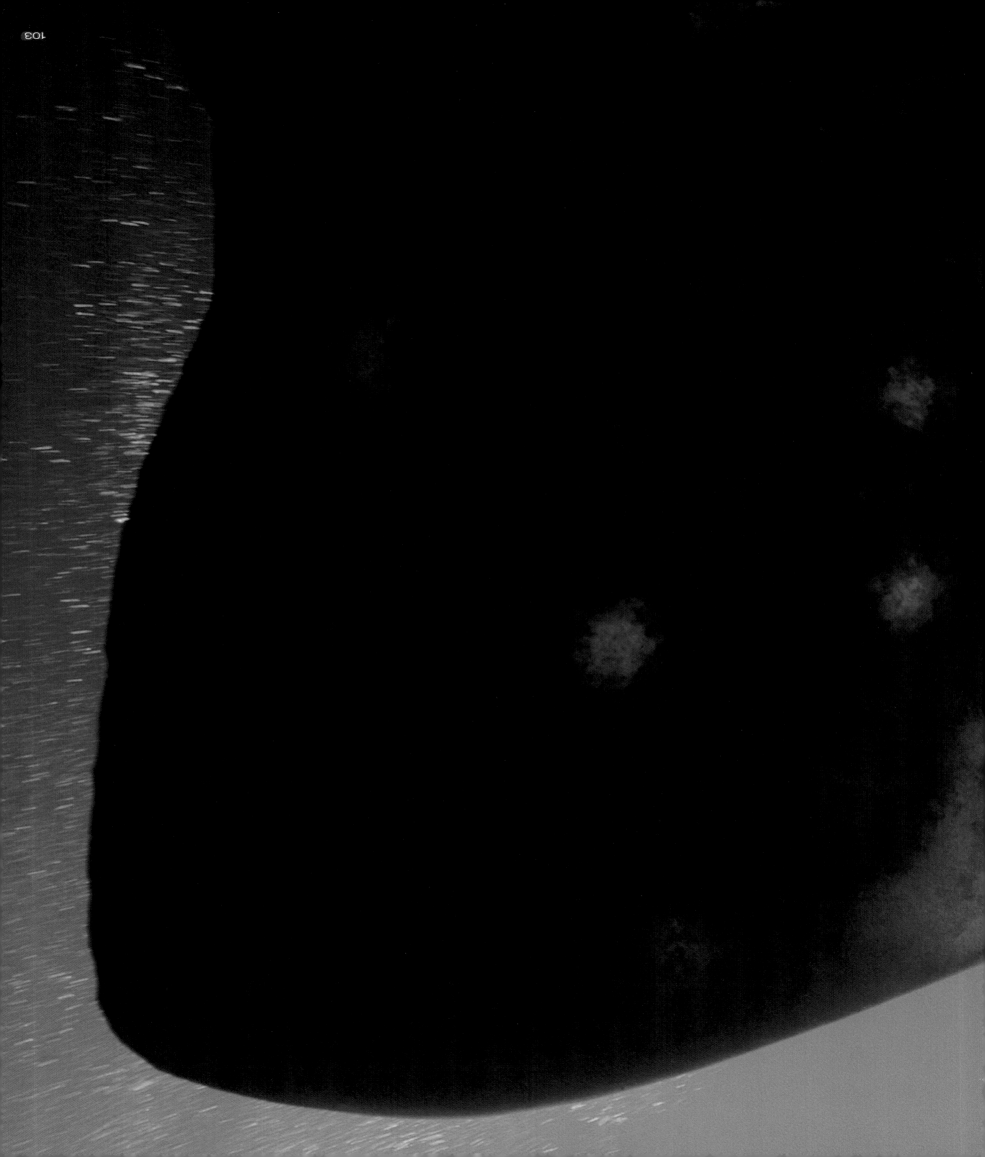

Rays & Skates

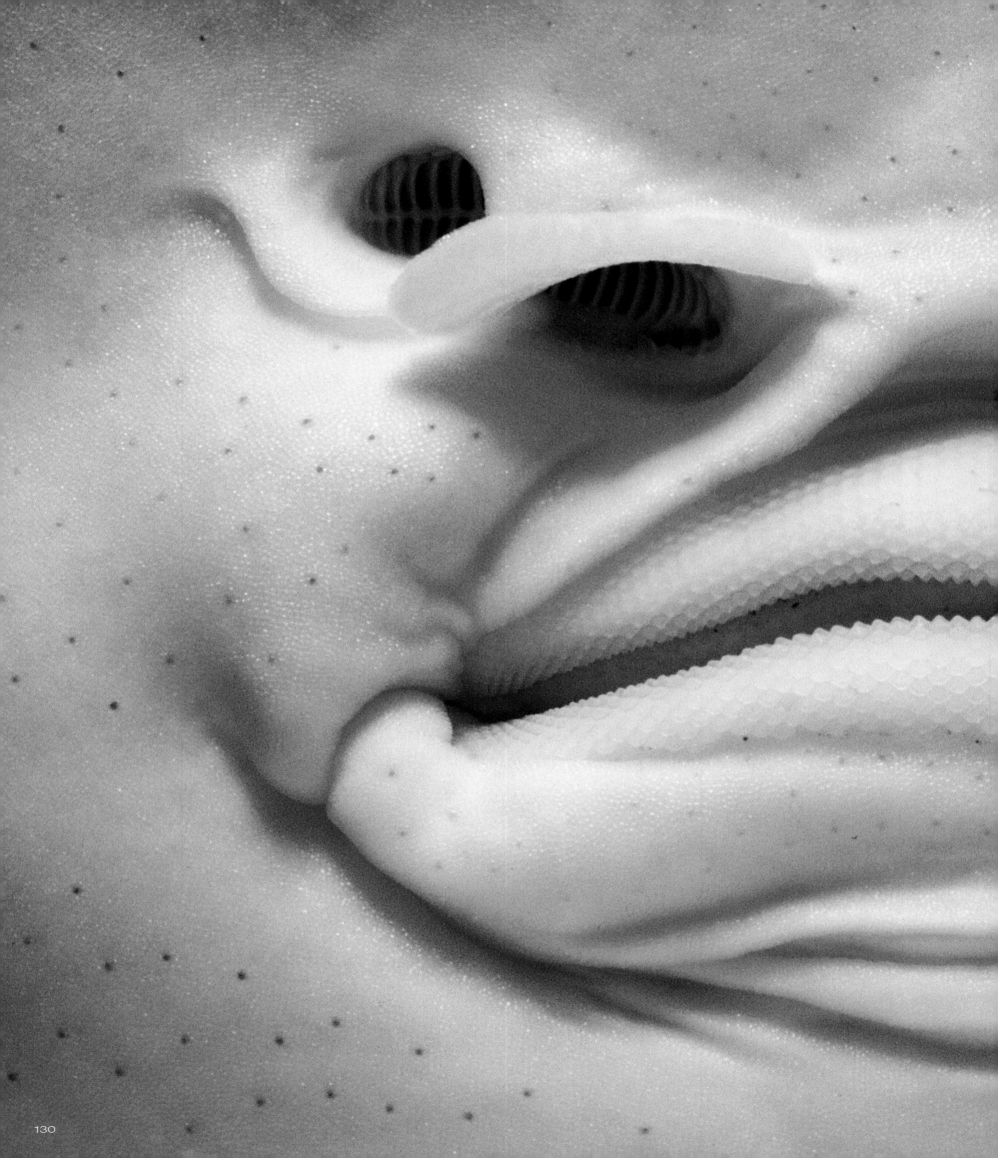

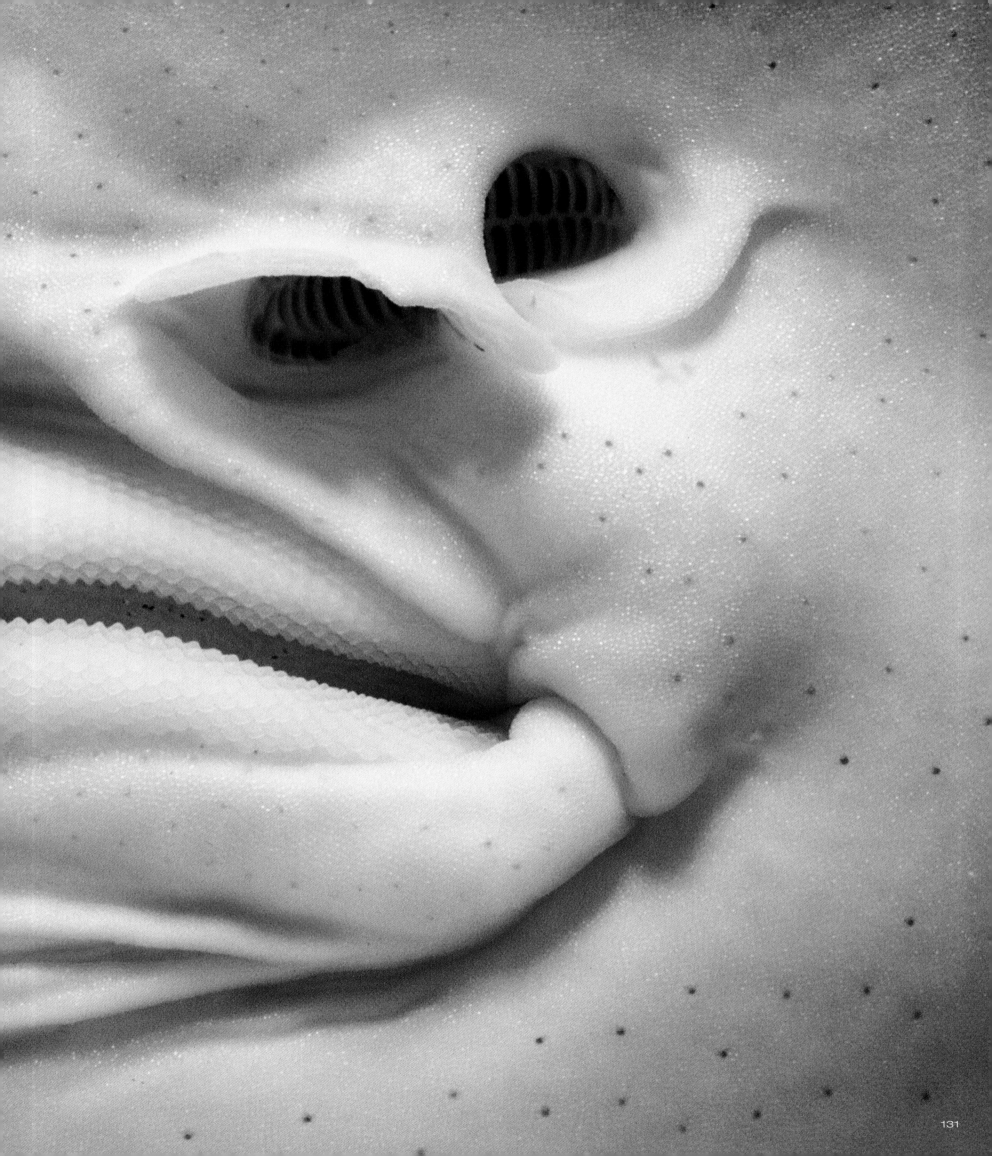

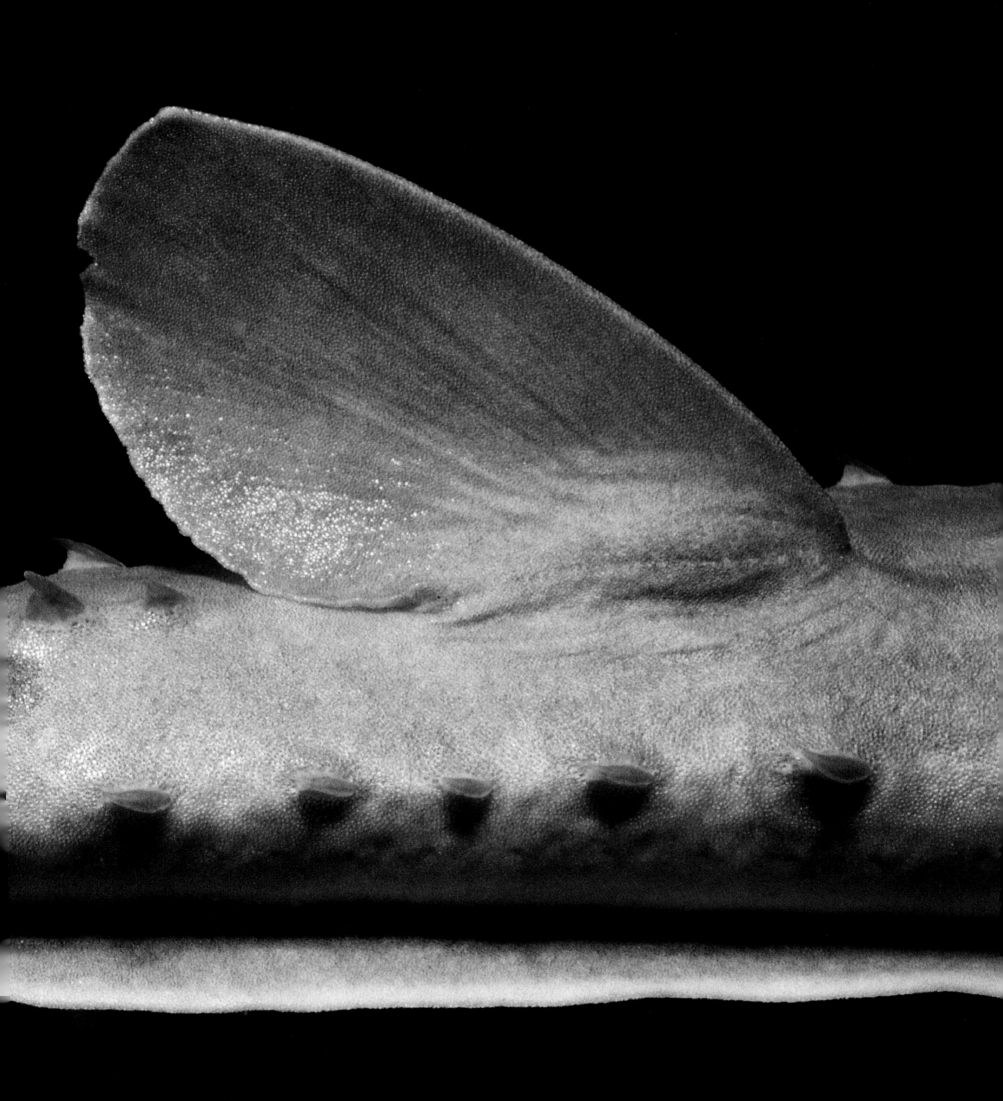

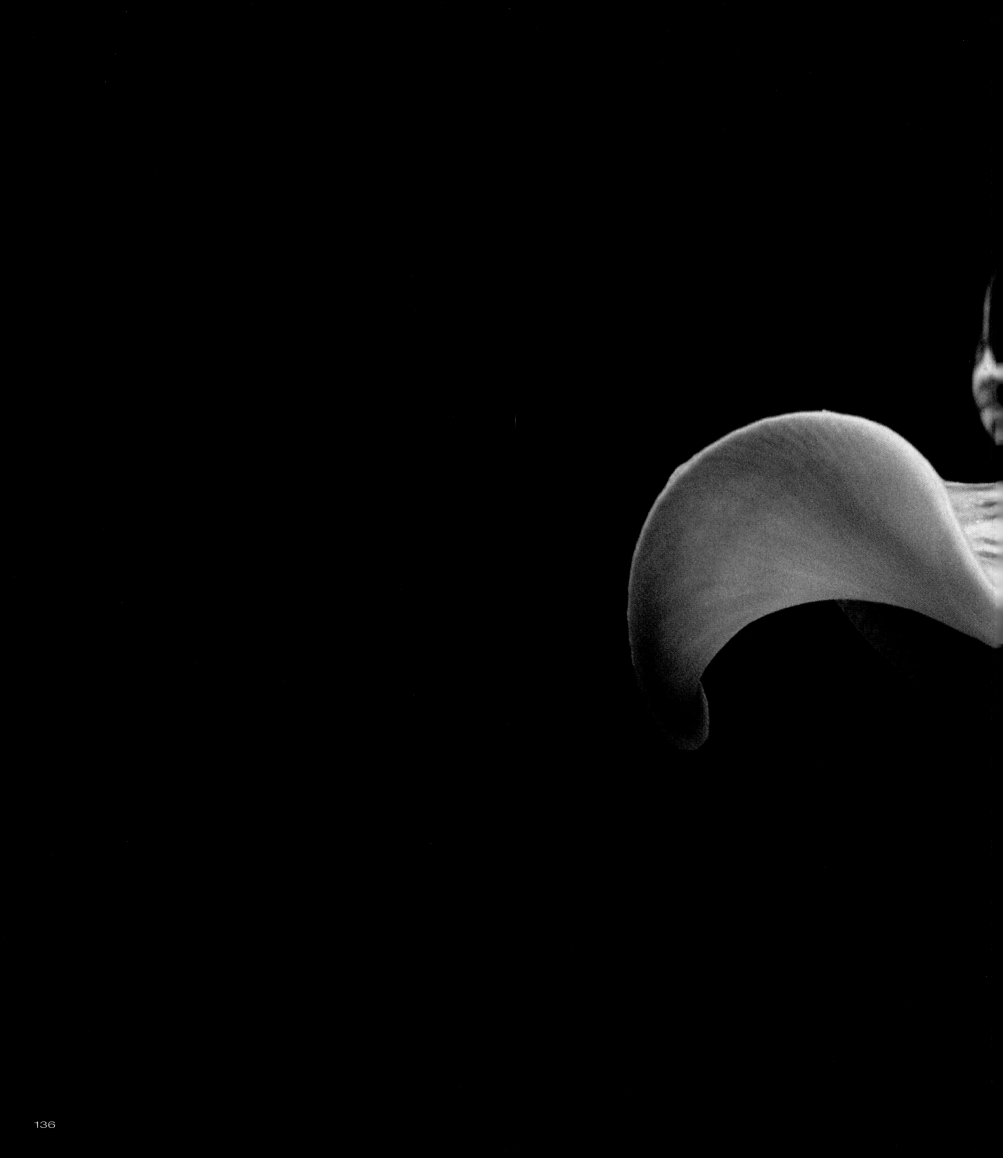

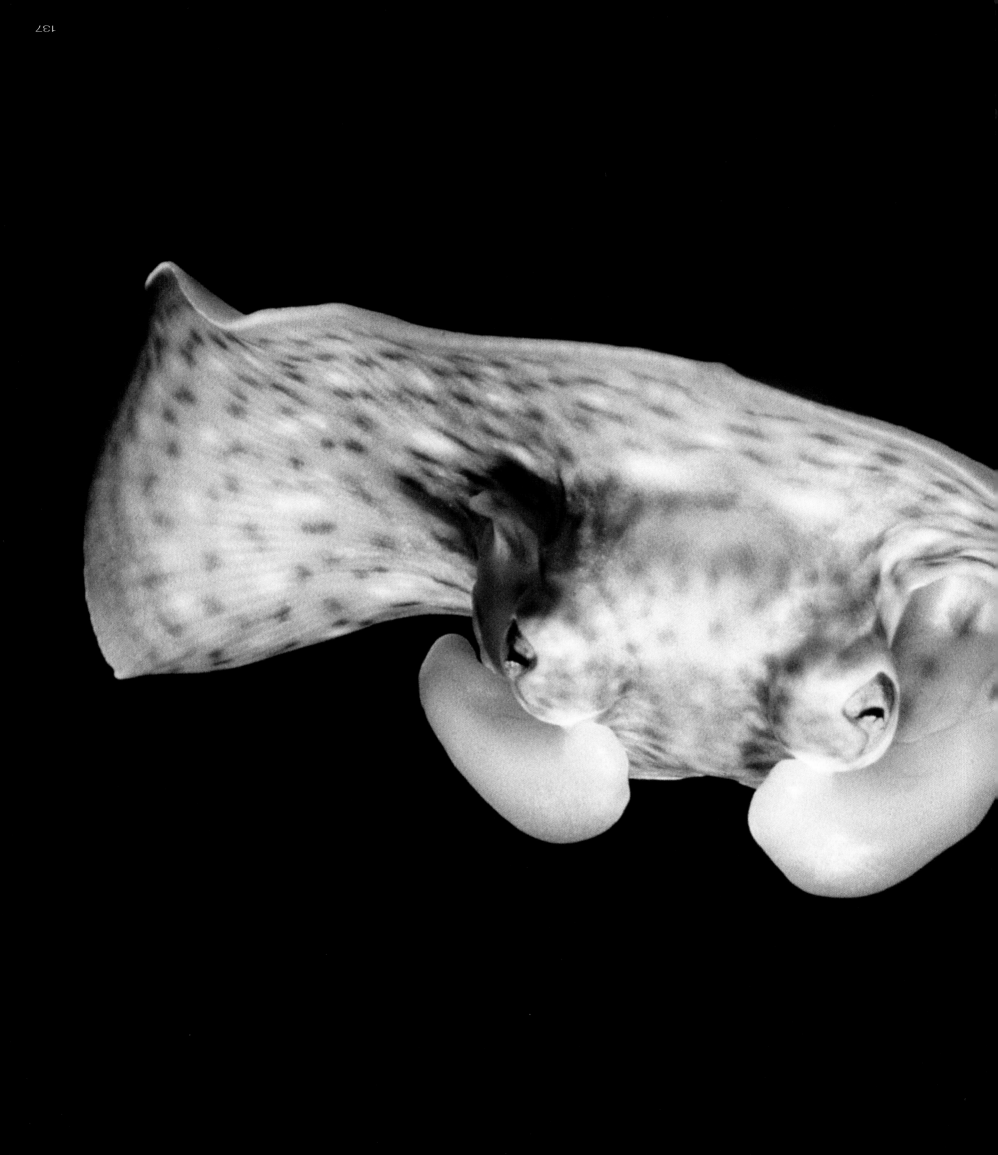

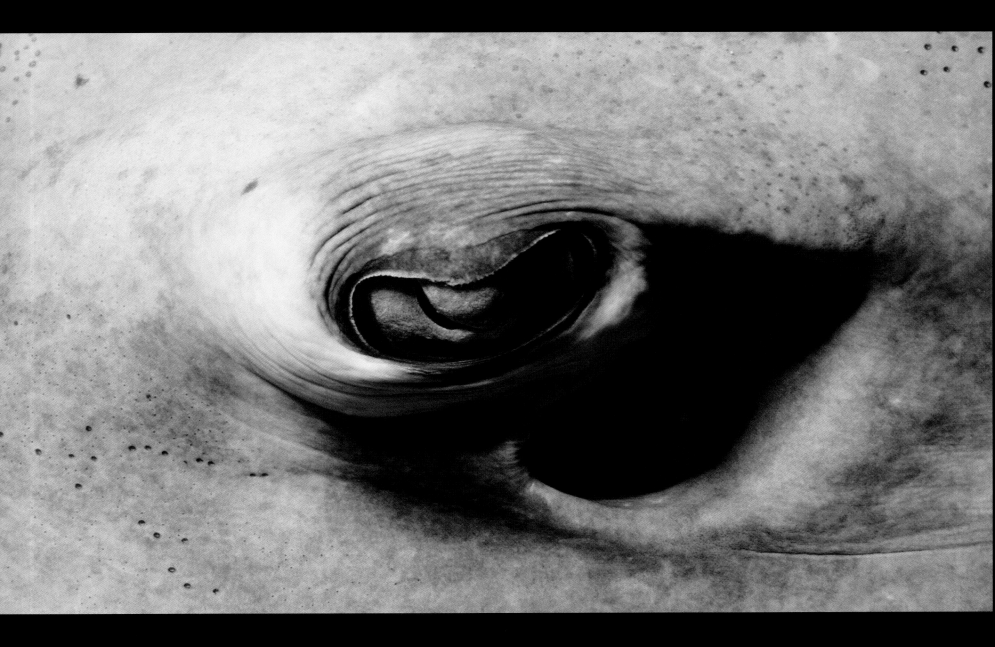

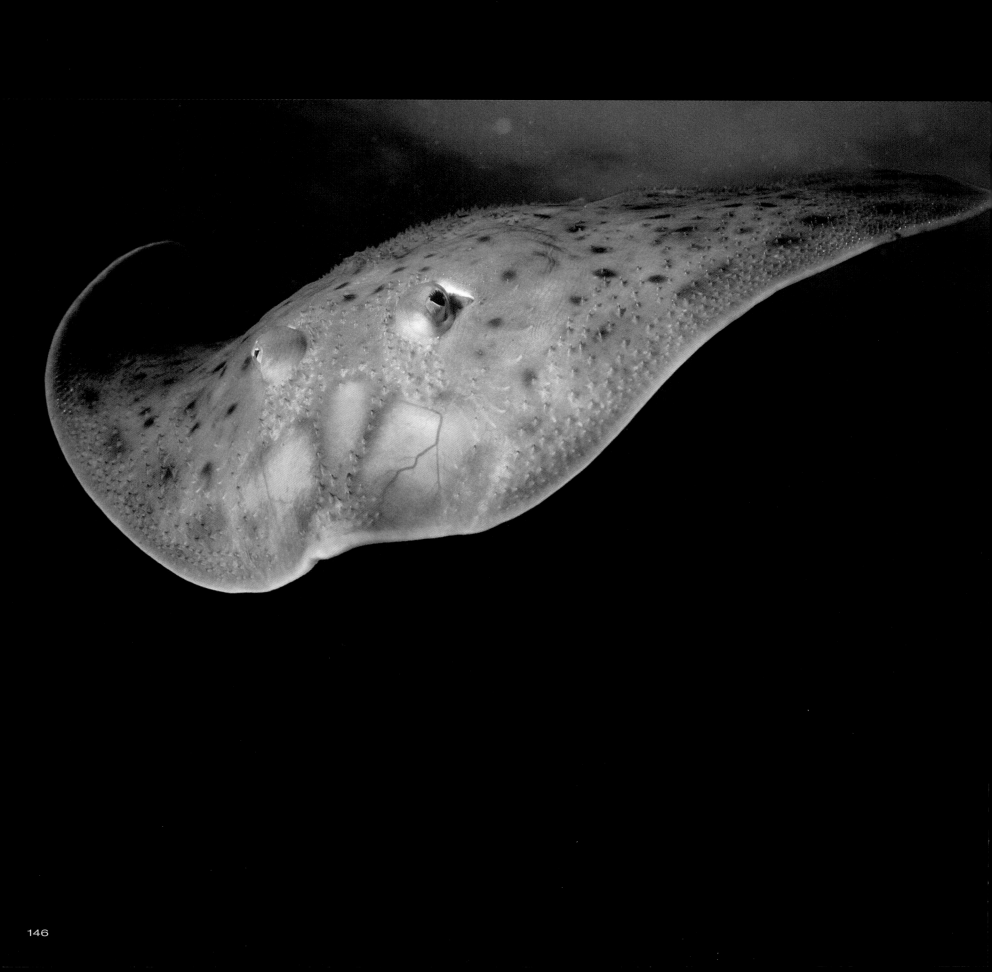

Feeding & Handling

Sharks in Danger

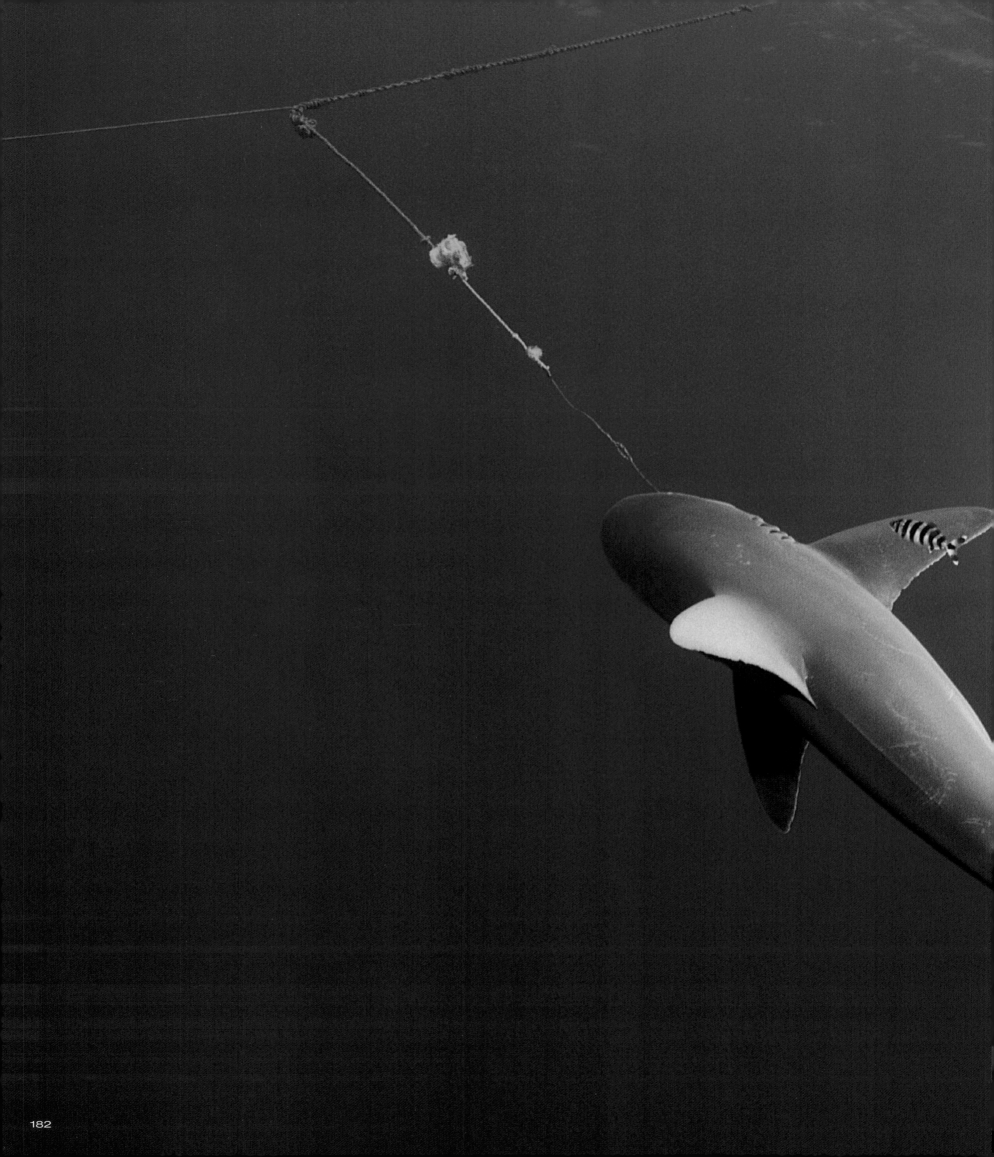

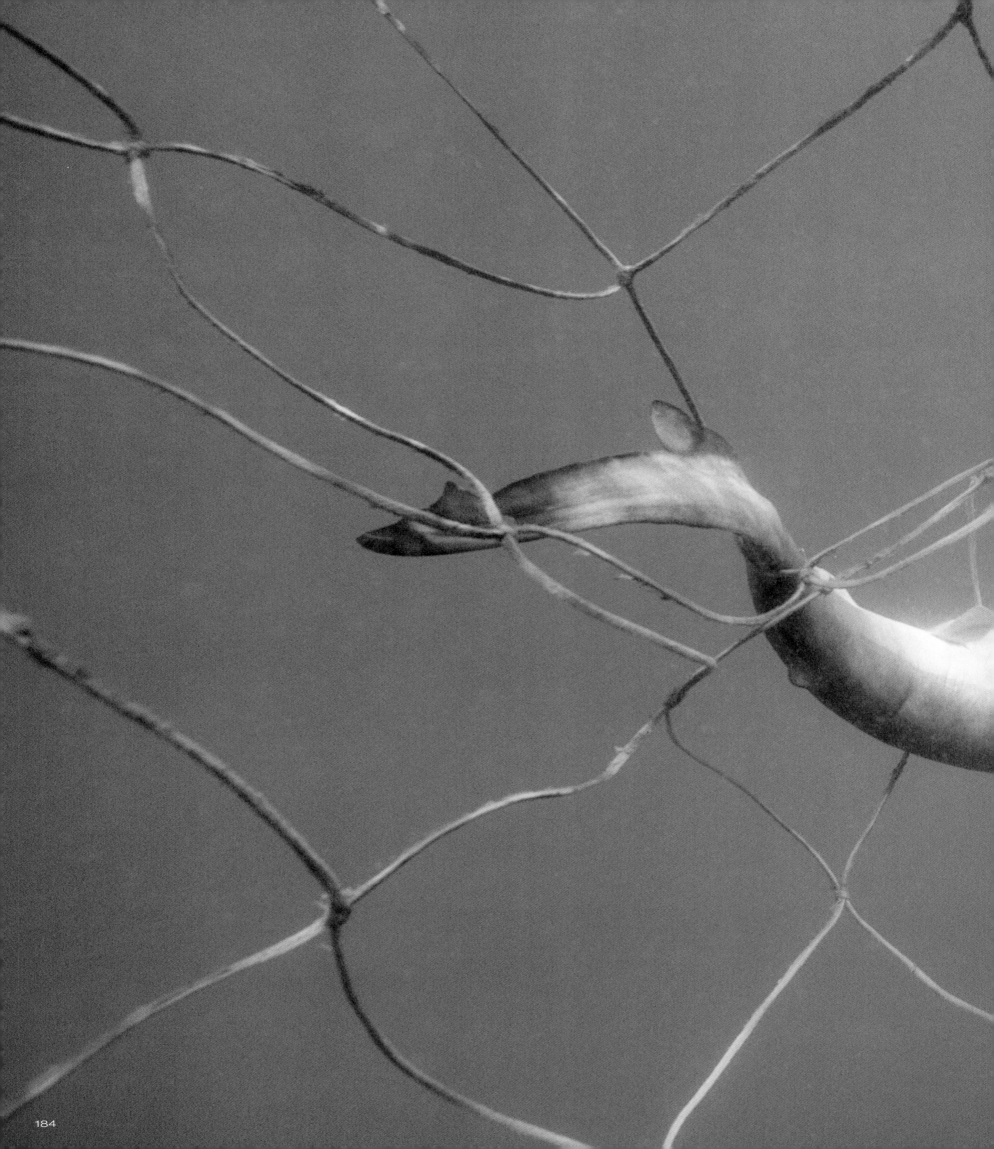

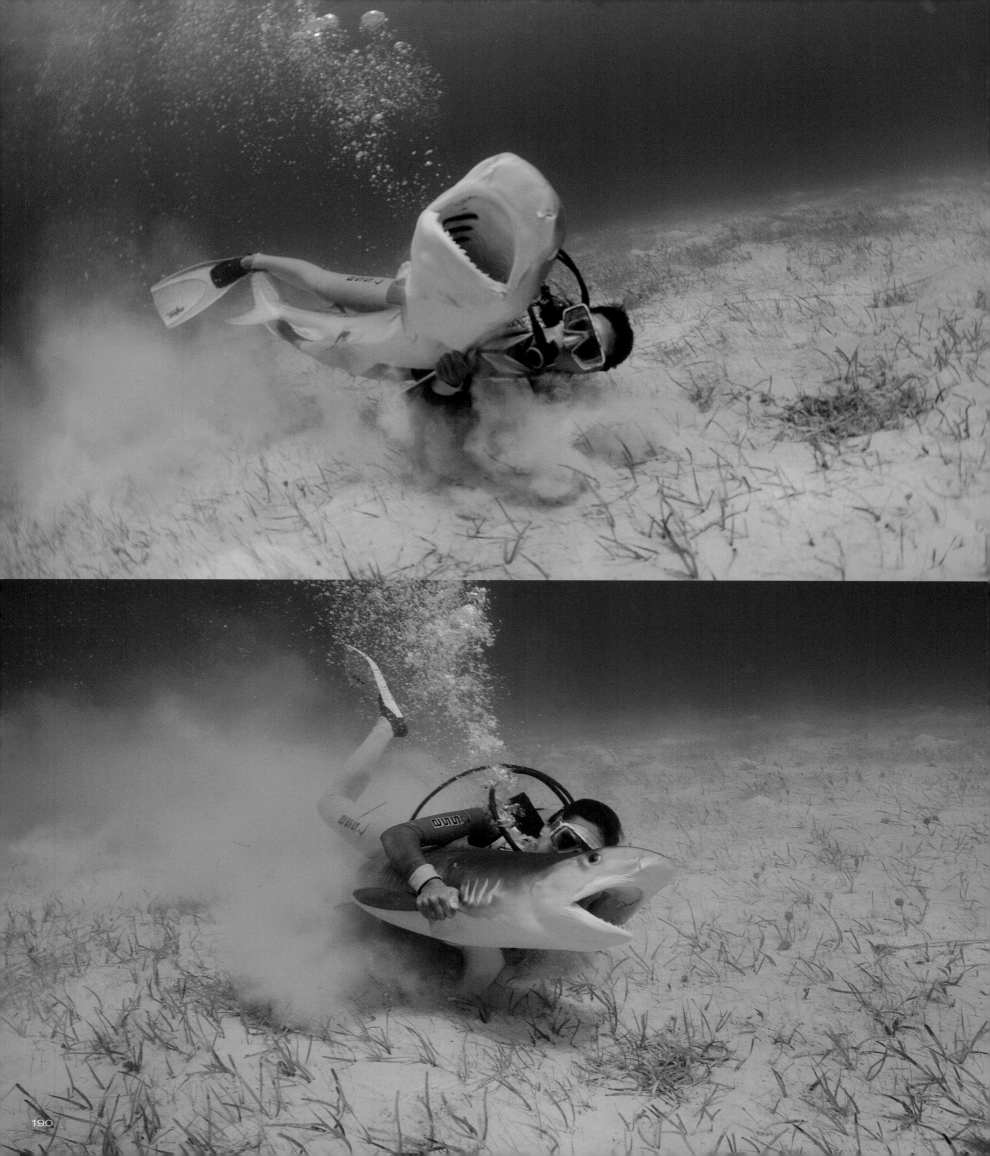

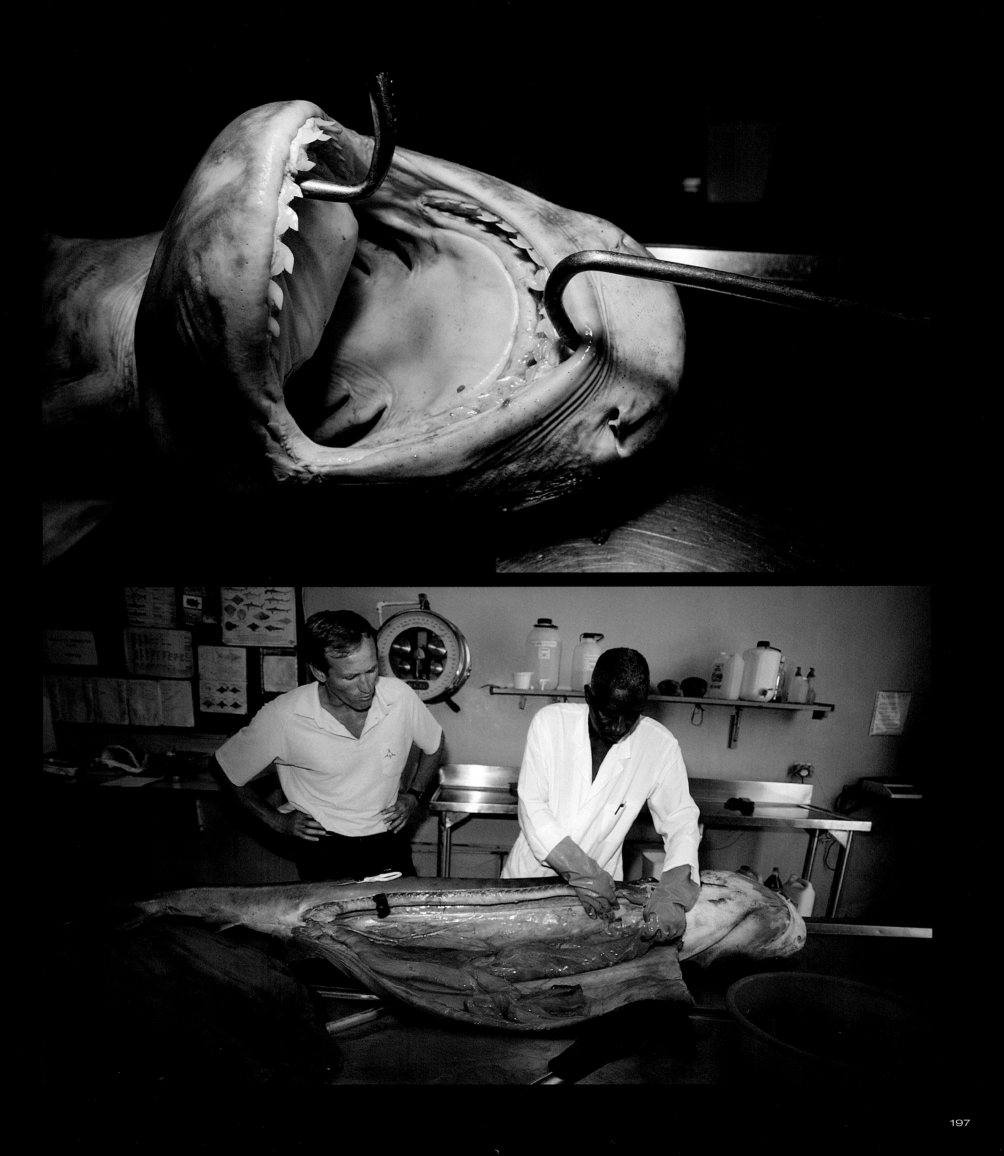

Index

Cover Sand Tiger Shark
Eugomphodus taurus, North Carolina, USA.
If looks could kill...we'd die of fright. The toothsome sand tiger shark fits the image of the ultimate predator, but it is actually a gentle animal. This photo illustrates a shark behavior called yawning; in the case of the sand tiger, its jaws widen to terrifying proportions, which I was lucky enough to capture on film.

P. 02 Swellshark
Cephaloscyllium ventriosum, San Clemente Island, California, USA.
Many rows of pointed teeth are the signature feature of sharks, making even the smallest sharks effective predators. This California swellshark lies in rocky crevices waiting to ambush unsuspecting fish and crabs. If attacked, it can gulp water to blow itself up to the size of a beachball.

P. 04 Caribbean Reef Shark
Carcharhinus perezi, Freeport, Grand Bahama Island.
Who's afraid of whom? Experienced shark diver Ben Rose seems to have the situation well in hand as he examines the teeth of a Caribbean reef shark. Even Ben would not be so bold if he were not wearing a protective chainmail shark suit.

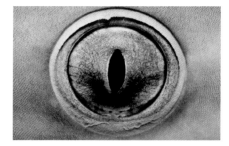

P. 06 Whitetip Reef Shark
Trianodon obesus, Gulf of Aqaba, Red Sea.
The unblinking eyes of a shark are adapted for the low light of the ocean. Some sharks have a light-reflective layer that greatly improves their vision in dim light. This natural reflective mirror, similar to those in cats' eyes, gives their eyes an eerie glow when caught by the beam of a diver's lamp.

P. 10 Caribbean Reef Shark
Carcharhinus perezi, Nassau, Bahamas.
Jeff Rotman in action! A shark feeder passing out free fish quickly attracts a crowd of Caribbean reef sharks. This near-perfect photo opportunity can only happen by offering handouts, intentional or otherwise. These sharks become accustomed to being fed morsels by hand at certain locations near tropical resorts. They often show up at the same time and place every day even before the tourist dive boats arrive!
© Photo courtesy of Asher Gal

ONE IN THE SEA

P. 15 Blue Shark
Prionace glauca, San Clemente Island, California, USA.
A long, slender body of indigo blue above and stark white below identifies this animal unmistakably as a blue shark. During World War II, its distinctive elongated snout, large eyes, and pointed pectoral fins were the last sight many downed pilots and sailors saw. This species was responsible for many of the shark attacks that plagued sinking ships during the war.

P. 16 Zambezi Shark
Carcharhinus leucas, Durban, Natal Coast, South Africa.
The Zambezi shark lives close to shore, sometimes too close. This individual was found in only a few meters of water off the Natal coast of South Africa. The species is infamous for swimming hundreds of kilometers upriver. Common and unwelcome in both coastal waters and fresh water, Zambezi sharks have been implicated in more shark attacks than any other species of tropical shark. Scientists suspect that many attacks on humans attributed to the great white shark were really the work of this shark.

P. 18 Great White Shark
Carcharodon carcharias, Dangerous Reef, South Australia.
Once you see Mr.Big you can never forget him. The great white is definitely the "Cadillac" of sharks. It is not the length, but the girth, personality and power this fish commands that makes it the king of sharks. Great whites are not the mindless eating machines of "jaws" fame. Far from it. Recent studies have shown that they are very particular about what they bite into with a strong preference for pinnipeds that have a high fat content. Great whites probably favor fat because they burn prodigious amounts of calories.

P. 20 **Tiger Shark**

Galeocerdo cuvier, Nassau, Bahamas.

This tiger shark nearly drowned when it was hooked by a long line. If it can't swim, it can't breathe. Shark handler Michelle Cove walks the shark in circles to force oxygenated water over its gills to revive it. This is a very courageous act of kindness since tiger sharks have been known to attack humans.

P. 22 **Caribbean Reef Shark**

Carcharhinus perezi, Freeport, Grand Bahama Island.

The reef shark is the star of many shark feeding demonstrations staged for tourists. After receiving instructions to keep their hands to themselves, scuba divers seeking a once-in-a-lifetime experience are seated on the ocean floor at a depth of 12 meters. The shark feeder arrives shortly after with a metal container filled with fish which he or she passes out to sharks eagerly waiting for a free meal. While not particularly aggressive, Caribbean reef sharks have been known to attack divers, especially when bait or speared fish are involved.

P. 24 **Whitetip Reef Shark**

Trianodon obesus, Gordon Reef, Gulf of Aqaba, Red Sea.

Despite its streamlined shape, this whitetip reef shark is not an effective open-water hunter. It is primarily a bottom feeder, using its short, broad snout to corner prey against reef crevices, where they cannot escape. Like most reef sharks, it may fall prey to other,larger sharks or to giant groupers.

P. 26 **Caribbean Reef Shark**

Carcharhinus perezi, Nassau, Bahamas.

Countershading -dark above and light below- is a feature that helps camouflage the shark as it sneaks up on its prey. The shark's excellent senses of feeling, hearing, and smell enable it to locate its quarry from a great distance. Its speed and stealth help it close in for an attack without alerting its prey until it is too late to escape.

P. 28 **Southern Stingray**

Dasyatis americana, Grand Cayman Island, Caribbean.

Rays are sharks whose fins and body have merged into a flattened disk. The mouth and gills are on the underside. Southern stingrays are favorite foods of sharks so it is important for them to conceal themselves. Generally they bury themselves almost completely in the sand; only their eyes protrude. Apart from their camouflage, a poisonous barb at the base of their tail is their only defense. In Grand Cayman, southern stingrays have been hand fed for years, so they are very friendly, even pestering, to divers and snorkelers.

P. 30 **Manta Ray**

Mantas birostris, Revillagigedo Islands, Mexico (Pacific).

Free diver Terry Maas gets the ride of a lifetime as a giant manta ray carries him 20 meters below the surface. Here near Socorro Island, 500 kilometers off the coast of Cabo San Lucas, Mexico, humans and mantas have developed an amazing relationship. The great rays actually approach divers, stop and allow them to climb onboard. With a flap of their wings, they whisk their passengers on a magic carpet ride through the blue sea.

CLOSE-UPS

P. 34 **Scalloped Hammerhead Shark**

Sphyrna lewini, Kane'ohe Bay, Hawaii.

If a shark has a soul, it is in its eyes. They draw you to it, as the eyes of this juvenile scalloped hammerhead did me. Its eyes are unusually large in comparison to its body. As it matures, it will grow into those eyes as it approaches its maximum length of 3-4 meters. Hammerheads are considered dangerous to humans. More curious and aggressive than most sharks, hammerheads are one species I would never turn my back on. Although I am cautious, I have never had an incident with this species, even when surrounded by a large school of them. However, a friend of mine was battered by a large hammerhead which seemed intent on eating his camera housing.

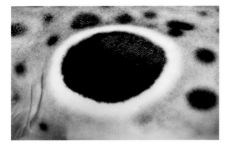

P. 36 **Epaulette Shark**

Hemiscyllium ocellatum, Papua New Guinea.

At a half meter in length, the small epaulette shark needs all the help it can get to avoid becoming an appetizer for a larger shark. The mottled skin of this shark helps to camouflage it against the ocean floor of a coral reef or sandy lagoon. It has large black splotches just in front of its gill slits. Perhaps to a potential predator, these spots may look like the giant eyes of an invincible opponent.

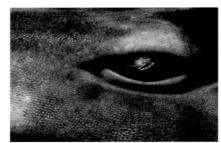

P. 38 **Swellshark**

Cephaloscyllium ventriosum, Santa Cruz Island, California, USA.

My dive buddy spotted a meter-long swell shark during a night dive in 1978 off Santa Cruz Island, California. At his approach, it wedged itself between two boulders and inflated itself to nearly twice its normal size. This made it appear more formidable to a potential predator. If that doesn't discourage an attacker, it at least makes it harder to swallow.

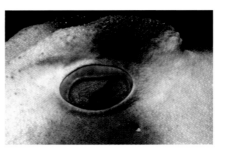

P. 40 **Port Jackson Shark**

Heterodontus portusjacksoni, Jervis Bay, New South Wales, Australia.

The eye is the hardest part of a fish to disguise. Many coral reef fishes sport a band of color that runs right through the eye, but this feature is unusual in sharks. This disruptive coloration breaks up the body pattern and camouflages the eye. A band of darker shading incorporates the shark's eye into its color scheme. This Port Jackson shark is nearly a twin to the California hornshark on page 44.

P. 42 **Tiger Shark**

Galeocerdo cuvier, Coral Sea, Australia.

A 3-meter-long tiger shark in the Coral Sea of Australia continuously harassed my safety diver Asher Gal. He had to fend it off repeatedly with a homemade shark billy. Each time he poked it away, the shark automatically closed its nictitating membrane, making this image possible. Fish do not, as a rule, have eyelids, but sharks often defy fish convention. Many species of sharks have a special adaptation called a nictitating membrane that closes over the eye during an attack to protect this vulnerable organ from the bones and teeth of its prey.

P. 43 **Caribbean Reef Shark**

Carcharhinus perezi, Freeport, Grand Bahama Island.

A mile off the coast of Freeport, Bahamas, shark handler extraordinaire Neal Watson grabbed this Caribbean reef shark and put it into a trance-like state. It lay motionless in his arms except for the flickering of its nictitating membrane. Despite the fact that Neal wears a protective chainmail anti-shark suit, this is a maneuver that should only be attempted by very experienced shark feeders.

P. 44 **California Hornshark**

Heterodontus francisci, Santa Rosa Island, California, USA.

When I first started exploring the ocean over 2 decades ago, it was relatively easy to find a California hornshark. Recently it took me a week of night dives to find one specimen off the northern Channel Islands, where I had found more than a dozen California hornsharks in years past. What had changed? Was it the effect of a recent El Niño, a change in the habitat, or overfishing? Whatever the cause, I believe it is evidence that the biodiversity of the ocean is decreasing.

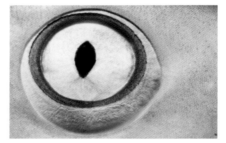

P. 46 **Lemon Shark**

Negaprion brevirostris, Bimini Island, Bahamas.

The eyes of sharks have always fascinated me. Some, like this lemon shark, have black pupils like cat's eyes, while in other species the black fills the entire orb.

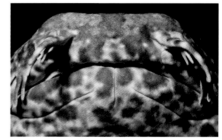

P. 48 **Wobbegong Shark**

Orectolobus maculatus, Jervis Bay, New South Wales, Australia.

All I saw was mouth when I came across this wobbegong shark lurking on a sandy shoal off eastern Australia. Fleshy lobes of skin fluttering in the current help lure hapless victims while the shark itself lies motionless on the ocean floor. When the prey comes close enough, the wobbegong darts out of the sand and vacuums it into its cavernous mouth.

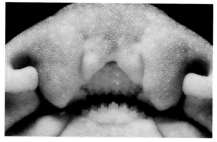   

P. 50 California Hornshark

Heterodontus francisci, Santa Rosa Island, California, USA.
The grinding teeth of this California hornshark reveal its preference for armored prey such as mollusks, crabs and sea urchins. Its taxonomic name meaning mixed-tooth refers to the fact that the pointed teeth near the front of its mouth grade to blunter teeth near the back. The convoluted nostrils of the hornshark enable it to detect microscopic levels of chemicals in the water.

P. 52 Epaulette Shark

Hemiscyllium ocellatum, Kimby Bay, Papua New Guinea.
Sharks are different from other fishes in that they have internal fertilization. A shark's clasper serves the role of a penis. Having two claspers, as this male Epaulette shark has, does seem to be redundant, however. Perhaps that is what scientists mean when they refer to sharks as primitive fishes!

P. 54 Velvet Belly Shark

Etmopterus spinax, Israel, Mediterranean.
This embryonic siny shark was aborted from a pregnant female when its mother was pulled up from the ocean floor during a deep-sea expedition off the coast of Haifa, Israel. Had it been able to grow to adulthood, it would have eventually reached a length of 20 centimeters, making it among the smallest species of sharks.

P. 56 Moses Smoothhound Shark

Mustellus mosis, Gulf of Aqaba, Red Sea.
This deep-water shark was captured at 500 meters off Eilat, Israel. It was raised to the surface in stages over 3 hours. This allowed it to decompress slowly in order to adapt to the tremendous change in pressure from its natural habitat. Once it reached the surface, divers swam the shark in circles to force oxygenated water over its gills. The shark survived its ordeal. The Moses smoothhound shark is well adapted for life on the deep ocean floor. A bottom feeder, its nostrils are on its ventral (bottom) side to help it locate prey living on the ocean floor. Its eyes have extremely powerful reflectors that maximize the dim light reflecting off potential prey.

   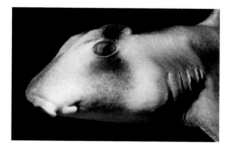

P. 58 Sand Tiger Shark

Eugomphodus taurus, Seal Rocks, New South Wales,Australia.
This fearsome-looking beast is a popular exhibit in public aquariums because its protruding, dagger-like teeth provide the spine-chilling thrill visitors seek. It adapts easily to captivity and will willingly take food from divers, which also makes it popular with aquarists. In the wild, divers sometimes encounter large aggregations of sand tiger sharks in offshore waters, probably pursuing their primary diet, schools of fishes.

P. 60 Upper left:
Velvet Belly Shark

Etmopterus spinax, Israel, Mediterranean.
Full-grown at 20 centimeters, the small size of this female siny shark probably is a consequence of the limited food supply in the deep ocean where this shark lives.

P. 60 Lower left:
Bigeye Houndshark

Iago omanensis, Gulf of Aqaba, Red Sea.
What big eyes you have! Another deep ocean dweller is the bigeye houndshark. This animal's large eyes take advantage of the small glimmer of light that penetrates to the depths of the Red Sea.

P. 61 Upper right:
Port Jackson Shark

Heterodontus portusjacksoni, Jervis Bay, New South Wales, Australia.
Ridges above the eyes of this Port Jackson shark give it a surprised expression.

P. 61 Lower right: **Epaulette Shark**

Hemiscyllium ocellatum, Kimby Bay, Papua New Guinea.
The epaulette shark is a member of the carpetsharks, named for their bottom-dwelling lifestyle. Looking at this specimen's rough hide could make you think it owed its name to the rug-like texture of its skin, which is covered with dermal denticles.

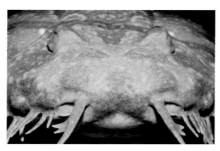

P. 62 **Wobbegong Shark**

Orectolobus maculatus, Jervis Bay, New South Wales, Australia. The wobbegong shark is so confident of its convincing camouflage that it refuses to budge even when it has been discovered. I slowly inched toward this animal until I was less than a third of a meter from its face. Only after I repeatedly assaulted it with explosions of light from my flash did it finally disengage itself from the ocean floor and wriggle away.

P. 64 **Scalloped Hammerhead**

Sphyrna lewini, Kane'ohe Bay, Hawaii.
There is no mistaking a hammerhead shark with its broad, flat head that looks like it had been squeezed in a vise. What is the advantage of this feature? Widely-spaced eyes and nostrils may make the hammerheads senses more acute than those of other sharks. The flattened head also may add lift and improve swimming efficiency.

P. 66 **Sand Tiger Shark**

Eugomphodus taurus, Seal Rocks, New South Wales, Australia. Its threatening countenance may be one reason that sand tiger sharks have been favorite targets of spearfishing divers. This species is now protected from further slaughter in New South Wales, Australia. Sand tiger sharks have become a tourist draw in New South Wales, South Africa, the United States, and Japan, where scuba divers can safely approach and photograph these terrifying-looking creatures. Although a sand tiger may occasionally make a determined move that causes a diver to give it space, humans need not fear being attacked by this gentle species.

P. 68 **Sand Tiger Shark**

Eugomphodus taurus, North Carolina, USA.
What look like freckles on this sand tiger shark are actually extremely sensitive electrical receptors called ampullae of Lorenzini after a 17th-century researcher, Stephan Lorenzini, who thought the shape of these tiny, jelly-filled pores resembled the jars (ampullae) used by the ancient Romans. All living things give off an electrical aura from pumping hearts and beating gills. These sensory organs, unique to sharks, detect these weak electric currents, even in animals buried under the sand.

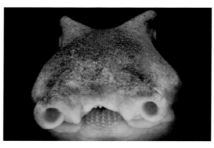

P. 70 **Port Jackson Shark**

Heterodontus portusjacksoni, Jervis Bay, New South Wales, Australia.
What could be more engaging than this whimsical portrait of a Port Jackson shark with its coiled nostrils and raised brows? Its mouth seems to open in a winsome smile that makes you almost want to pet this shark.

P. 72 **Caribbean Reef Shark**

Carcharhinus perezi, Walkers Cay, Abaco, Bahamas.
Even at a distance sharks create an overwhelming presence, but when one is this close, you appreciate every nuance of its visage: the pinprick holes of the ampullae of Lorenzini, the thin line of its mouth, the small protuberance of its nostrils, and, of course, its alert and absorbing eyes.

P. 74 **Whitetip Reef Shark**

Trianodon obesus, Gordon Reef, Gulf of Aqaba, Red Sea.
This whitetip reef shark is a bottom feeder and its developed nostrils greatly help it find molluscs and crustaceans. Sharks have an amazing olfactory sense, most species can detect blood in concentrations as low as one part per ten millions.

P. 76 **Whitetip Reef Shark**
Triaenodon obesus, Coral Sea, Australia.
Diving in pristine waters 200 kilometers from shore, I encountered this young whitetip on a night dive in the Coral Sea, beyond the Great Barrier Reef. This whitetip has the perfect, blemishless skin of youth. As a shark ages, its skin becomes scarred by its aggressive or amorous encounters with other sharks. It may have been my imagination, but this young shark seemed more cautious of me than an older specimen would have been.

P. 78 **California Hornshark**
Heterodontus francisci, Santa Rosa Island, California, USA.
I found this animal at night, resting in a shallow cave of boulders in about 4 meters of water. The hornshark typically rests among large rocks in kelp beds during the day and forages for food at night. As I passed my dive light across its body, the spine just in front of its dorsal fin sprang to attention. If another animal tries to swallow the hornshark, this characteristic spine makes it a painful passage down the throat; usually the predator disgorges the shark instead.

GIANTS

P. 82 **Basking Shark**
Cetorhinus maximus, Isle of Man, Irish Sea.
I spent weeks scanning the waters surrounding the Isle of Man waiting for this sight. This dorsal fin heralded the arrival of the annual summer migration of basking sharks to the Irish Sea. Basking sharks, the second largest fish in the sea, come here each summer to feed on the rich planktonic soup. As soon as I spotted the fin, we jumped into a small zodiac and quietly approached the feeding behemoth. I slipped into the water without air tanks in order not to distract it from its meal.

P. 84 **Great White Shark**
Carcharodon carcharias, Dangerous Reef, South Australia.
First contact! Nothing can prepare you for your first encounter with a great white shark. It looks directly at you as it passes by, giving you the distinct impression that it is sizing you up. Many other sharks attack at dawn or dusk, but the great white's eyesight is well adapted for daylight hunting, when its preferred prey, seals and sea lions, are also active.

P. 86 **Great White Shark**
Carcharodon carcharias, Dangerous Reef, South Australia.
February and March, summer Down Under, are the months to visit Dangerous Reef in southern Australia as that is when great white sharks visit, too. Elongated pectoral fins and an enormous girth distinguish the great white from all other sharks.

P. 88 **Great White Shark**
Carcharodon carcharias, Dangerous Reef, South Australia.
The only safe way to share the water with a great white shark is from inside a sturdy shark cage. As the shark gnaws at the bars of the cage, you question the cage's structural integrity. But the shark is probably just examining this strange presence, or perhaps the electrical field of the metal bars has excited its sensitive electric receptors. Either way, you fervently hope that your shark cage can withstand the attention.

P. 90 **Great White Shark**
Carcharodon carcharias, Dangerous Reef, South Australia.
Great white sharks are totally unpredictable. Some shark-watching expeditions wait two weeks without a sighting, returning home empty-handed. On our trip, we encountered the first of many great whites within five hours of our arrival. Over the next ten days, great whites were a constant presence. At times I was surrounded by as many as five.

P. 92 **Great White Shark**
Carcharodon carcharias, Dangerous Reef, South Australia.
Coal black eyes and gleaming white teeth is the image that people who have had a face-to-face encounter with a great white shark remember forever. Sunlight accents the five gill slits on the side of the great white shark. Rows of gill slits, a cartilaginous skeleton, and many rows of teeth distinguish sharks and rays from all other fishes, called bony fishes.

P. 94 **Great White Shark**

Carcharodon carcharias, Dangerous Reef, South Australia.
Luckily, perhaps, most victims never get to see this nightmarish ventral view of a great white shark. A great white usually strikes from below so most victims never see what hit them. According to shark specialist John McCosker, great whites tend to sneak up on their prey, take a massive bite, and then back off until the victim bleeds to death. McCosker calls this theory "bite and spit" behavior, believing that this allows the shark to avoid being gored by the claws and tusks of the struggling animal.

P. 96 **Great White Shark**

Carcharodon carcharias, Dangerous Reef, South Australia.
A strongly-built, streamlined body tapering to a broad forked tail show that this shark is capable of traveling long distances in search of food. Great whites are thought to roam the world's oceans, but they are only protected from being killed by conservation laws in South Africa, Australia, and parts of the United States.

P. 98 **Whale Shark**

Rhincodon typus, Ningaloo Reef, Western Australia.
At a length of 14 meters, the whale shark is not only the largest shark in the sea, it is the largest fish as well. Most open-water sharks are countershaded, but the whale shark has a distinctive color pattern. This shark cruises slowly near the surface, pursued by divers, as it strains shrimp-like krill from the seawater. I had to move directly into its path in order to get this photo taken from a distance of 3 meters. All the other whale sharks I approached would veer away before I could get this image. This one was like watching a freight train bearing down on me, and I hoped we'd avoid impact at the last second. Fortunately the whale shark altered its course.

P. 100 **Whale Shark**

Rhincodon typus, Ningaloo Reef, Western Australia.
Ningaloo Reef is one of the few places in the world where you are guaranteed to see whale sharks. Even there they only frequent the area for a few months; in April and May, when the upwelling of nutrient-rich water from the deep ocean encourages the growth of plankton. A spotter plane locates the whale shark and directs our boat to the general location. The captain tries to drop us off in the path of the oncoming shark as it is impossible to catch up to them once they pass by. These remoras, on the other hand, have no trouble keeping up with these giants of the sea.

P. 102 **Whale Shark**

Rhincodon typus, Ningaloo Reef, Western Australia.
This is the largest dorsal fin you will ever see in the ocean. After waiting 20 years for a chance to meet this goliath, I couldn't resist hitching a ride on its fin. I hung on with my left hand as I shot photographs with my right. The shark carried me down to 35 meters before I had to let go when my pony tank registered close to empty. I snapped this parting shot as it continued to dive and I slowly retreated to the surface after the ride of my life. Today, conservation laws no longer allow people to touch whale sharks at Ningaloo.

P. 104 **Whale Shark**

Rhincodon typus, Ningaloo Reef, Western Australia.
The skin on the back of the whale shark is extremely thick and tough, while its belly is made of a much softer tissue. It only allows divers to approach its tougher side. Notice the mobility of the pectoral fins which allow this massive animal to change direction effortlessly.

P. 106 **Whale Shark**

Rhincodon typus, Ningaloo Reef, Western Australia.
Aware of our presence, a whale shark would allow us to keep up with it for a hundred meters or so. Should it feel threatened, a quick thrust of its tail shoots it right past you. If you happen to be in the path of that flick, it has the power to knock you into the next ocean.

P. 108 **Whale Shark**

Rhincodon typus, Ningaloo Reef, Western Australia.
Like a living reef, the whale shark is often accompanied by smaller fish, like this golden trevally, that either seek refuge in its shadow or forage for leftovers. The whale shark feeds on shrimp-like plankton, small fish, and occasionally, larger ones.

P. 110 Basking Shark

Cetorhinus maximus, Isle of Man, Irish Sea.

Possibly even rarer than the whale shark, the basking shark prefers cooler temperate waters that are rich in plankton. The plankton clouds the water like an underwater fog, reducing visibility to a few meters at best. Add to this the rain and clouds above the surface, and photographing basking sharks in the Irish Sea becomes a trying, soggy venture. Guiding me in these waters was Ken Watterson, the director of the Basking Shark Society, who has spent most of his life learning about these beasts.

P. 112 Basking Shark

Cetorhinus maximus, Isle of Man, Irish Sea.

To photograph feeding basking sharks you have to get close enough to see through the murky water but be careful not to spook these timid creatures. We did not use scuba gear so they would not be disturbed by the bubbles and the noise of the regulators. A basking shark is basically toothless, catching plankton on sticky gill rakers as it slices through the water with its mouth wide open.

P. 114 Basking Shark

Cetorhinus maximus, Isle of Man, Irish Sea.

Even though you know it only feeds on minute plankton, the size of a basking shark's enormous mouth is daunting. Sightings of 10-meter-long basking sharks lolling at the ocean's surface inspired legends of sea monsters by ancient mariners.

RAYS & SKATES

P. 118 Pacific Cownose Ray

Rhinoptera steindachneri, Isla Darwin, Galapagos Islands.

Early morning and late afternoon are magical times on the reef, when a sudden swarm of marine life can transform the sea into a city at rush hour. A school of Pacific cownose rays in flight formation was my reward for entering the sea at sunrise. I watched in awe, too stunned to react. Finally I managed to squeeze off a few shots before the squadron disappeared into the blue.

P. 120 Manta Ray

Manta birostris, Revillagigedo Islands, Mexico (Pacific).

The giant manta ray is a bizarre filter feeder plowing through the water with its mouth wide open to capture small animals on its gill rakers. Ancient mariners called it the devilfish, but its horns are actually extended cephalic lobes that funnel plankton toward its mouth. A gentle giant, the manta ray can grow to weigh over a ton with a wing span of 5 meters.

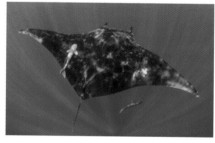

P. 122 Manta Ray

Manta birostris, Revillagigedo Islands, Mexico (Pacific).

Mantas occur throughout the tropics, near shore as well as in the open sea. They are well suited to the open ocean and probably swim continuously. Here at a depth of ten meters this manta swims above a kilometer of blue water. A rare combination of crystal clear water and a calm sea surface allowed me to capture this animal contrasted against the impossibly blue water of the deep ocean.

P. 124 Manta Ray

Manta birostris, Revillagigedo Islands, Mexico (Pacific).

A view from below shows that the gills of a manta, as with all rays, are on its underside. It also reveals its delicate, white underbelly, a striking contrast to its dorsal side which is protected by sandpapery skin. Here off Socorro Island, the mantas are accustomed to free divers (breathholding divers without scuba) so they allow us to see their vulnerable side.

P. 126 Manta Ray

Manta birostris, Revillagigedo Islands, Mexico (Pacific).

When we came across these manta rays, I was onboard a boat full of blue water hunters in search of world-record tuna and wahoo. When they encountered these gentle creatures, the hunters put aside their spear guns to frolic with the mantas. I am not sure which species enjoyed it more. A free diver would team up with a manta and hang on like a sucker fish as the ray dove down to 30 meters for 2 minutes or longer. As soon as the free diver left the manta, the ray would circle back and come alongside, inviting him to grab hold for another ride.

P. 128 Manta Ray
Manta birostris, Revillagigedo Islands, Mexico (Pacific).
Two sucker fish have the best seats in the house, anchored by their suction cups to the lobes that shepherd small fish and plankton into the ray's mouth. Here they are well positioned to take advantage of any leftovers.

P. 130 Thornback Ray
Platyrhinoidis triseriata, Santa Cruz Island, California, USA.
A face only a mother could love! The underside of this ray shows its tiny grinding teeth which can grip a crab or mollusk firmly before crushing its shell.

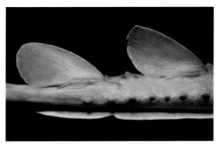

P. 132 Thornback Ray
Platyrhinoidis triseriata, Santa Cruz Island, California, USA.
This thornback ray has rows of thorny spines to discourage predators from making a grab for it. The tail of this ray is a splendid piece of marine engineering with its double rudder and keel on the underside.

P. 134 Thornback Ray
Platyrhinoidis triseriata, Santa Cruz Island, California, USA.
Thornback rays rest in small groups in the sand during the day and venture out at night to feed. That is when I caught up with this specimen and accompanied it for the better part of an hour. Periodically it would tire of my flashing strobe and try to bury itself in the sand, only to discover that its camouflage did not work with me.

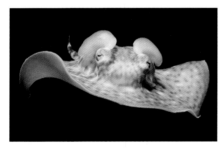

P. 136 Yellow Stingray
Urolophus jamaicensis, Freeport, Grand Bahama Island.
This little fellow was born before my eyes. In the late afternoon I encountered a female yellow stingray wriggling in the sand. Over the course of the next half-hour, six palm-sized babies emerged. Fully formed, though miniature, each one immediately swam away to lead an independent life. Rays reproduce in two ways: by live birth as this mother did, or by laying eggs. The familiar mermaid's purse is the leathery egg case of the skate, another group of rays. Rays have long gestation periods and relatively small litters, so they are vulnerable to overfishing and destruction of their habitats.

P. 138 Yellow Stingray
Urolophus jamaicensis, Freeport, Grand Bahama Island.
The gills on the underside of the yellow stingray expand and contract to help pump water through its respiratory system. This allows the animal to remain motionless on the ocean floor and still get enough oxygen to survive. The pores around its gill openings are tiny sensory pits that feed information to the animal's brain.

P. 140 Southern Stingray
Dasyatis americana, Grand Cayman Island, Caribbean.
In this photo, professional underwater model, Isabelle Delafosse, is surrounded by southern stingrays. They don't really love her, but they do love the squid juice I rubbed all over her wet suit! In Grand Cayman, stingrays have been conditioned to expect food from humans. They began showing up on a regular basis about 25 years ago when local fishermen started cleaning their catch and throwing the remains overboard into a shallow bay near the stingrays' feeding grounds. Today that broad bay, now called Stingray City, is a major tourist draw. As explicit as a dinner gong, the sound of an approaching motorboat engine summons up to 70 stingrays at a time. One can snorkel or dive among hordes of stingrays that nuzzle up to you for a handout of squid. You can even hold them and pet them; just take care not to tread on their barbed tails.

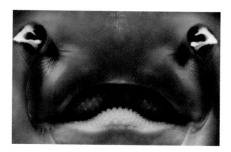

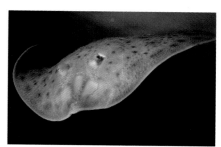

P. 142 > 143 **Southern Stingray**
Dasyatis americana, Freeport, Grand Bahama Island.
Rays are fascinating creatures from head to tail. The poisonous barb is constructed like a fish hook, with backward-pointing spines that make them difficult to extract. The eyes are located on

the top of its head just in front of spiracles, which take in ocean water for breathing. If it took water in through its mouth, as most fish do, it would ingest sand each time it breathed, because all but its eyes are usually buried under the sand.

P. 144 **Little Skate**
Raja erinacea, Folly Cove, Cape Ann, Massachusetts, USA.
During the spring months, skates such as this one pepper the bay and coves of coastal New England. I have seen the bottom of coves covered with these remarkable creatures. They scour the ocean floor for anything pala-table. Its mouth is a wonder of design, equipped to crush and grind a rock crab, quahog clam, or blue mussel.

P. 146 **Little Skate**
Raja erinacea, Folly Cove, Cape Ann, Massachusetts, USA.
When not lying motionless in the sand, skates and rays turn into flying saucers, propelling them-selves through inner space.

P. 147 **Javanese Cownose Ray**
Rhinoptera javanica Kimby Bay, Papua New Guinea.
When you work at night in a pitch black sea, and your torch exposes a javanese cow-nosed ray, you immediately stand up and take notice. The cover of darkness seems to offer the more vulne-rable rays and skates the protec-tion they need to avoid being eaten in a predator-filled ocean.

P. 148 **Spotted Eagle Ray**
Aetobatus narinari, Durban, Natal Coast, South Africa.
Nose to nose with the spotted eagle ray, which is found along tropical coastlines and in muddy bays. It comes inshore daily to feed on buried shellfish which it excavates by beating its wings near the bottom and then grabs and crushes it between its strong teeth plates.

P. 150 **Blue-spotted Stingray**
Taeniura lymma, Orens Reef, Gulf of Aqaba, Red Sea.
When I first started diving in the northern Red Sea in 1972, this blue-spotted stingray was ubiqui-tous in certain areas. Far fewer of these beautiful creatures grace these waters today, casualties of unregulated, intensive develop-ment along the Sinai Peninsula.

FEEDING & HANDLING

P. 154 **Caribbean Reef Shark**
Carcharhinus perezi, Freeport, Grand Bahama Island.
The desire to get close to sharks, for photography or for research, spurred the development of the chainmail antishark suit in the 1980s. It afforded protection from sharks (some sharks) without repelling or harming them as most other antishark devices did. Made of thousands of inter-locking stainless steel links (at a cost of about $8,000), the heavy suit allows the wearer to handle small to medium sharks. To a large predator such as a great white shark or a tiger shark, however, the suit would probably just taste slightly crunchy!

P. 156 **Caribbean Reef Shark**
Carcharhinus perezi, Freeport, Grand Bahama Island.
Keep your hands folded on your lap, advises Neal Watson to the divers who accompany him on a shark feeding. Never one to heed his own advice, Neal has wrestled wild sharks for fun and profit, for TV commercials and in action films. For the past several years, Neal has organized shark feeding ventures around the Caribbean. Although thousands of tourists have taken part, no one yet has been injured.

P. 158 **Caribbean Reef Shark**
Carcharhinus perezi, Freeport, Grand Bahama Island.
In the Bahamas and other parts of the Caribbean, shark watching has become a major spectator sport. Having sharks swarm around you like bees around a hive is an exhilarating experience. My safety diver, Asher Gal, enjoyed being the center of attention for these eager suitors instead of having to beat them away from my back as he has had to do in tenser situations in the open ocean.

P. 160 **Caribbean Reef Shark**
Carcharhinus perezi, Freeport, Grand Bahama Island.
Even relatively inexperienced divers can watch the action in safety. Neal Watson, a record-holding diver for most of his 50 years, remembers when he had to reassure scuba diving clients that they would not meet a shark; now he has to guarantee that they will!

P. 162 **Caribbean Reef Shark**
Carcharhinus perezi, Freeport, Grand Bahama Island.
Neal Watson introduces his two sons, Neal and John D., at ages 12 and 13, to the pleasures of shark watching. Veteran divers since they were practically toddlers, both boys love going to work with Dad.

P. 164 **Caribbean Reef Shark**
Carcharhinus perezi, Freeport, Grand Bahama Island.
Like synchronized swimmers, these Caribbean reef sharks circle in close formation around veteran shark handler Ben Rose. These sharks, like most sharks, are not particularly large. Caribbean reef sharks average a meter and a half in length, although some grow to 3 meters. Except for those acclimated to commercial shark feeding, most retreat from divers. Getting close to these sharks generally requires patience.

P. 166 **Nurse Shark**
Ginglymostoma cirratum, Walkers Cay, Abaco, Bahamas.
At Walker's Cay in the Bahamas, shark feeding is more of a free-for-all. Fish heads frozen into a large ball are suspended by a chain. Sharks attack the bait from every direction. They battle the frozen mass with their bodies, tearing off large chunks of bait with every bite. As the excitement builds, as many as 100 sharks may be attracted to the feast. In contrast, the hand-feeding of sharks is, by necessity, a more disciplined affair.

P. 168 **Caribbean Reef Shark**
Carcharhinus perezi, Walkers Cay, Abaco, Bahamas.
Curiosity overcomes caution as this Caribbean reef shark comes in for a close-up. As it scrutinizes me, its downturned mouth, so characteristic of sharks, gives the impression it doesn't like what it sees. An ingrained survival mechanism warns a shark to avoid anything as big as or bigger than itself. When a shark encounters a diver, its first instinct (and perhaps the diver's) is to retreat. In order to get close enough to photograph a shark, it is necessary to overcome its natural fear of us.

P. 170 **Caribbean Reef Shark**
Carcharhinus perezi, Walkers Cay, Abaco, Bahamas.
If there is a typical shark it is the reef shark, like these Caribbean reef sharks. Sleek and swift, reef sharks patrol large areas of reef and some species are thought to be very territorial. Nonetheless, the Caribbean reef shark welcomes shark-feeding divers into its domain.

P. 172 **Caribbean Reef Shark**
Carcharhinus perezi, Freeport, Grand Bahama Island.
Look into my eyes! Some people believe the magnetic field created by the metal links of the chainmail suit can disrupt a shark's electromagnetic sense and put it into a brief trance-like state.

P. 174 **Caribbean Reef Shark**
Carcharhinus perezi, Freeport, Grand Bahama Island.
By offering a fish to this reef shark you bring it one step closer to a level of comfort which may allow it to go into a state of semi-sleep that results in the shark-handler being able to "handle" the shark.

P. 174 > 175
Caribbean Reef Shark
Carcharhinus perezi, Freeport, Grand Bahama Island.
Like a stage hypnotist, a diver takes advantage of the shark's stupor to make it perform embarrassing acts that it would never do if it were fully awake!

P. 175

P. 176 **Caribbean Reef Shark**
Carcharhinus perezi, Walkers Cay, Abaco, Bahamas.
No one would dare to encroach on the grace and dignity of this large female Caribbean reef shark. It is the chance to meet majestic creatures like this one that draws visitors to shark diving resorts.

SHARKS IN DANGER

P. 180 **Tiger Shark**
Galeocerdo cuvier, Coral Sea, Australia.
This 3-meter tiger shark was caught on a fishing line and released. Unfortunately, this is not usually the case. Many people who catch sharks, even accidentally, would prefer to see them die rather than return them to the ocean. Our fear of sharks is so great that we brought many species close to extinction. The large so-called man-eaters, such as tiger sharks and great white sharks, are especially threatened by trophy hunters.

P. 182 **Sandbar Shark**
Carcharhinus plumbeus, Israel, Mediterranean.
During the summer months sandbar sharks off the Mediterranean coast of Israel migrate inshore to mate and breed. Longlines are baited to catch them, and local fish markets do a brisk business in sandbar sharks during their mating season.Like most sharks, sandbar sharks grow slowly, mature late, and produce only a few pups in each litter. It takes a female sandbar shark off the coast of North America about 16 years to reach maturity. She gives birth to 8-12 pups, depending on her size, after nearly a year of gestation.

P. 184 **Smooth Hammerhead Shark**
Sphyrna zygaena, Durban, Natal Coast, South Africa.
A juvenile hammerhead is the latest victim of the shark net. Anti-shark nets have ringed the swimming beaches around the Natal coast of South Africa since 1952. The good news is there are rarely shark attacks here; the bad news is that entire populations of sharks have been decimated. A growing understanding of the importance of sharks in maintaining the biodiversity of the ocean are calling some to question the wisdom of this devastating practice.

P. 186 Sand Tiger Shark
Eugomphodus taurus, Durban, Natal Coast, South Africa.
What looks like a fierce maneater is actually just a harmless species with a serious overbite. This gentle sand tiger shark caught in the Durban antishark net primarily feeds on small animals like small sharks, rays, other fishes, crustaceans and squid. The Natal Sharks Board is mindful of the mortalities of non-dangerous sharks in the nets that protect the recreational beaches of KwaZulu-Natal. The Board is researching methods of reducing these mortalities without jeopardizing human safety.

P. 188 > 189 Tiger Shark
Galeocerdo cuvier, Nassau, Bahamas.
We stared into the crystal blue Bahamian waters and saw the irresistible outline of a good-sized shark silhouetted against the bottom. As we dove down to investi-gate, we realized the animal was pinned to the ocean floor by a large hook through its jaw. Shark expert Michelle Cove surfaced and returned immediately with a wire cutter to free the young tiger shark.

P. 190 Tiger Shark
Galeocerdo cuvier, Nassau, Bahamas.
Nearly dead by the time she cut it free, Michelle walked the shark around to force oxygen-rich water across its gills, the shark version of mouth-to-mouth resuscitation. After a few minutes, the shark suddenly burst free from Michelle's grasp and with three powerful thrusts of its tail disappeared into the Caribbean waters with half the hook still attached.

P. 192 Lemon Shark
Negaprion brevirostris, Bimini Island, Bahamas.
Dr. Samuel Gruber, professor of marine biology at the University of Miami Rosenstiel School of Marine and Atmospheric Science, has spent much of his career gathering information on lemon sharks. By tagging his subjects he is learning more about their movements, behavior and longevity.

P. 194 Scalloped Hammerhead Shark
Sphyrna lewini, Kane'ohe Bay, Hawaii.
High-tech radio transmitters help track juvenile scalloped hammerheads. Researchers Chris Lowe and Kim Holland slide the transmitter into the shark's stomach through a thin PVC pipe. After a few days, the shark regurgitates the device, as it does other indigestible items it may swallow. The scientists track the expensive transmitter, retrieve it, and reuse it on new subjects. They have learned that the juvenile hammerheads in Kane'ohe Bay, Hawaii, take refuge in loose schools in deep, murky parts of the bay by day (perhaps to avoid larger sharks). At night the pups move onto patch reefs to hunt for gobies, parrotfish, wrasses and snapping shrimp. It is research like this that enables us to better understand the role of sharks in the ocean food web.

P. 195 Scalloped Hammerhead Shark
Sphyrna lewini, Kane'ohe Bay, Hawaii.
Did you ever make a shark go to sleep? It's called tonic immobility. With certain sharks, like this juvenile hammerhead, you can flip them upside down, and they become immobile for a minute - the shark goes "dead". It doesn't harm the animal and provides a unique experience for the person handling the shark.

P. 196 > 197 **Tiger Shark**
Galeocerdo cuvier, Durban, Natal Coast, South Africa.
Shark attacks are a very real fear in South Africa which reports

about 15 attacks a year. The 39 kilometers of beaches that are surrounded by nets off the Natal coast have created a nearly shark-free zone. In an average

year, the Natal Sharks Board in Durban, South Africa, catches 1,400 sharks in its shark-deterrent nets. This 2.5 meter tiger shark is being examined by Jeremy Cliff

and Patrick Mthembu. Each animal is autopsied to provide more data on the sharks that frequent this area.

P. 198 > 199 **SHARK DETAILS**
A male shark has two penises! Claspers pass the sperm into the female during internal fertilization. This **Bigeye Houndshark** *Lago omanensis,* was captured in the Red Sea at a depth of 500 meters.

These teeth belonging to a six-meter **Great White Shark** *Carcharodon carcharias,* illustrate the serrated teeth that allow the animal to saw off a large chunk of meat from its prey.

Two pups are encased in an embryo sac removed from a pregnant **Bigeye Houndshark** *Lago omanensis,* taken from the same location as the male.

This deep-sea **Velvet Belly Shark** *Etmopterus spinax,* was captured in 1,200 meters of water off Israel in the Mediterranean Sea during a research study of deep sea bottom dwellers. Though there are not many different kinds of animals found at that depth, those that can survive thrive in large numbers. This is one of the smallest sharks, measuring 20 centimeters in length.

P. 200 > 201
SHARK FISHING

Shark fishing has been a longstanding tradition in some countries, but over the past 15 years shark fishing has become a multimillion dollar industry worldwide, particularly for shark fin soup. Heavy fishing pressure has led to the commercial extinction of some species and a growing threat to all harvested species. Slow-growing sharks do not have the capacity to bounce back from this exploitation. Shots from shark markets in India, Israel, South Africa and Japan show the variety of species and products that are sold.

P. 202 > 203
SHARK DANGER
Top to bottom, left: A sign posted on the beaches of Australia warns of the danger of shark attacks.

Someone who understands that danger firsthand is **Rodney Fox,** perhaps the most famous shark attack victim. He displays the scars from an attack by a great white shark more than 30 years ago that paradoxically turned him into a shark conservationist.

At the Jaws Room at the Natal Sharks Board, more than 100 jaws of various species are kept on hand to help determine the type of shark involved in an attack. A curator holds up the jaws of a 6-meter great white shark.

This 2-meter reef shark was attacked by a much larger shark, possibly a bull shark. From the size of the bite it could be surmised that the attacker was in excess of 3 meters long. Although large, dangerous sharks still roam the ocean, there are fewer of them than ever before. Just as we are beginning to understand that sharks play a critical role in maintaining the health and balance of the ocean ecosystem, we are in danger of losing many species of sharks.

P. 222 **Spiny Dogfish Shark**
Squalus acanthias, Gloucester, New England USA.
This rare photograph shows a newborn spiny dogfish with its yolk sac still attached. Normally, by the time this baby shark would emerge from its mother, this internal food supply would have been absorbed. Possibly, this fetus was spontaneously aborted when its mother was netted by fishermen. Large schools of these small sharks are harvested for "fish and chips."

P. 226 **Great White Shark**
Carcharodon carcharias, Dangerous Reef, South Australia.
Sometimes you can come nose-to-nose with a great white without even getting into the water. Great whites often spy hop and poke their heads above water possibly to look for tasty sea lions sunning themselves on rocks. Another surprising behavior is that great whites, despite their considerable bulk, have been seen jumping completely out of the water in pursuit of prey.

Text by Jeffrey L. Rotman, with Mary Cerullo

For Isabelle

SHARK! is published by IPSO FACTO PUBLISHERS

© 1999 Ipso Facto Publishers.
Photographs © 1999 Jeffrey L. Rotman, Boston.

Concept : Marc Parent
Editorial assistant : Susanne Ricard-König
Art direction : Christian Kirk-Jensen
Reproductions : Gert Schwab / Steidl, Schwab Scantechnik
Printing and production : Steidl, Göttingen

Published in the United States by Ipso Facto Publishers Corp.

ISBN : 1-893263-02-9

web site : http://www.ipsofactobooks.com

Distribution in the United States by :
RIZZOLI INTERNATIONAL PUBLICATIONS
c/o VHPS
175 Fifth Avenue
USA-New York, NY 10010
Phone : ++(1) 800 488 5233
Fax : ++(1) 800 258 2769

IPSO FACTO PUBLISHERS are represented worldwide by :
MP BOOKLINE international
30, rue de Charonne
F-75011 Paris
Tel : ++(33) 1 55 28 35 35
fax : ++(33) 1 55 28 35 30
mpbookline@aol.com

Printed and bound in Germany.

ipso facto
PUBLISHERS • NYC